Baking with Stevia II

More Recipes for the Sweet Leaf

by Rita DePuydt

Published by Sun Coast Enterprises

ISBN 0-9656073-1-3
Library of Congress Catalog Card No. 98-090800
Printed in the United States of America

Sun Coast Enterprises
PO Box 262
Oak View, CA 93022

COVER DESIGN
Debi Spann
COVER PHOTOGRAPHY
Rita DePuydt
IMAGE EDITING
Tony Hallas

❦ ACKNOWLEDGEMENTS ❦

I would like to thank my family and friends for the terrific support they have given me through the writing and production of both my first and second recipe books, with a special thanks to my father and mother, George and Mary DePuydt and my constant friends Lyn Duguid and Doug Davis.

I also greatly appreciate the support of all the wonderful folks at Wisdom of the Ancients, including, James May, Steve May, Lisa Ashcroft and all the others who work hard everyday selling healthful products.

I am grateful for the friendship and professional help of Tony and Daphne Hallas. Thanks again to Wendy Fletcher for the use of her beautiful tableware for the photo shoot. Thank you to Debi Spann for her creativity and hard work in designing the cover. I'm also grateful to Shannon Welch for proofreading the book.

A big thanks to Laurie Hopkins, Abe Santini, and many others at the Kinkos in Ventura, California for their personal and conscientious service. I also appreciate the quality work of the Ojai Printing and Publishing Co.

And finally I want to thank all those who have purchased my first volume of recipes-all the plant nurseries, health food stores, herb companies, book stores, and individuals. I sincerely hope the book has been of some assistance to those in pursuit of better health.

Thank You

Dr. Julian Whitaker
Dr. Whitaker's Newsletter, December 1994

"Stevia...is not only non-toxic, but has several traditional medicinal uses. The Indian tribes of South America have used it as a digestive aid, and have also applied it topically for years to help wound healing. Recent clinical studies have shown it can increase glucose tolerance and decrease blood sugar levels. Of the two sweeteners (aspartame and stevia), stevia wins hands down for safety."

Dr. Daniel Mowrey
Director of the Mountainwest Institute of Herbal Sciences

"Few substances have ever yielded such consistently negative results in toxicity trials as have stevia. Almost every toxicity test imaginable has been performed on stevia extract (concentrate) or stevioside at one time or another. The results are always negative."

Robert C. Atkins, M.D.
From Dr. Atkin's *Health Revelations* Newsletter, April 1994

"Stevia has virtually no calories. It dissolves easily in water and mixes well with all other sweeteners...I use it myself in delicious homemade ice cream that is extremely low in carbohydrates."

❖ CONTENTS ❖

COOKIES AND BARS

PUDDINGS AND PIES

GELATIN DESSERTS

TOPPINGS AND SAUCES

FROZEN DESSERTS

❖ FOREWORD ❖

Stevia is the sweetener of the future! Now is the time to learn how to cook and bake with this incredible herb. Volume I of *Baking with Stevia* was the first real stevia cookbook to be written and published. It is certainly the best one produced to date. The recipes in Volume One all utilize stevia extract powder, a white crystalline powder named stevioside, that is extracted from the leaves of the stevia plant. Depending on brand quality it will be 200 to 300 times sweeter than sugar. Stevioside does not adversely affect blood sugar, and therefore, may be used freely by diabetics and hypoglycemics. It does not, however, offer the same health restorative benefits as does the whole leaf stevia, which besides being sweet, is remarkably nutritious.

Rita has done it again with *Baking with Stevia II: More Recipes for the Sweet Leaf.* Not only does this volume contain additional recipes using stevia extract (stevioside white powder), but whole leaf stevia as well. You will love these recipes. Best of all, when eating or drinking the foods and beverages you can be assured that stevia has made them more nutritious and better for the health and well-being of every member of your family. Many experts believe that stevia is the safest sweetener known to man.

Stevia is an incredible plant. It is not only safe to use, it is *good* for you and adds *no calories* to your food. It does not make you crave more of it, as do some artificial sweeteners. In fact, stevia reduces ones cravings for sweets and improves oral health. The leaves of a good quality plant are about 30 times sweeter than sugar. These recipes not only provide the wonderful natural sweetness of stevia but its marvelous healing benefits as well. When cooking with whole-leaf stevia products, it is important to be aware that stevia leaves from China are not as sweet and do not have the same delightful flavor as Paraguayan stevia. When using the stevia extract powder look for a brand that contains as least 90% steviosides.

I was pleased when Rita asked me to write the foreword to Volume II of her *Baking with Stevia* recipes. I have been using stevia daily since my introduction to it in 1982. I have worked continuously with both the Guarani Indian farmers and Paraguayan agricultural officials to improve both the quality and quantity of their Stevia production. I have importuned many congressmen and

1

other U.S. Government officials in order to increase the availability of this remarkable herb in America.

Stevia is one of Paraguayan herbs that has become my passion. I love stevia. I love its taste and what it does within the human body. I am especially partial to natural whole-leaf stevia products. I'm pleased that Volume II introduces recipes that use all the various forms of stevia. As you learn to use this remarkable herb, you too, will come to love it and be grateful for stevia and its numerous health restoring properties.

Uses for high quality ground Paraguayan stevia leaves are as varied as your imagination. Try it as a sweet spice on cooking vegetables and meats. Sprinkle it into soups, cereals, salads, barbecue and pasta sauces, stews and chili. Blend it with ground cinnamon for delicious cinnamon/stevia toast. Make your own sweet liquid from the stevia tea bags and use that in cooking or baking, or make ice cubes to sweeten other beverages. Children love a stevia Popsicle. Stevia makes good food better-and more nutritious! In addition to all of the sweet compounds, stevia leaves contain numerous vitamins and minerals, including beta-carotene, vitamin C, austroinulin (nourishes the good bacteria in our intestines), calcium, chromium, cobalt, iron, magnesium, manganese, niacin, phosphorus, potassium, protein, selenium, silicon, sodium, and zinc.

Where else will you find an herb, in its natural form, that is deliciously sweet but will nourish your pancreas and help to restore and maintain a normal blood sugar level and even help to lower high blood pressure? Where else will you find a sweet tasting herb that helps to destroy harmful bacteria, reduce cavities, and help to stop bleeding gums? Where else will you find such an herb, that in its natural liquid concentrate form, is as healing to the skin as it is to the internal body? When you discover some of the many uses and health benefits of the various forms of this sweet tasting herb it will become *your* passion. For the health of your family you will settle for nothing less than stevia. You will love Rita's stevia recipes and will soon be developing your own. Nature gave us this incredible plant. Enjoy the sweetness and health that is stevia.

James A. May, President
Wisdom of the Ancients

INTRODUCTION

Stevia rebaudiana

BAKING WITH STEVIA

In the first volume of *Baking with Stevia, Recipes for the Sweet Leaf,* a white powdered extract was used in all of the recipes. In this second volume, I introduce the cook to a number of other stevia products including: the dried green herb, a green liquid concentrate, and a clear liquid extract (see pages 9 and 10 for descriptions). Stevia is extremely useful and a health benefit in all of its forms.

The liquid and powdered stevia extracts are concentrates of the sweet tasting molecules known as glycosides that are found within the plant. These extracts are approximately 200-300 times sweeter than sugar. The whole green herb (dried), though less sweet than the extract, retains the medicinal attributes of the herb and contributes a pleasant sweetness to many foods. The herbal concentrate combines the medicinal properties of the whole herb (intensified) with a higher sweetening capability than the dried herb.

As with the first volume, this collection of recipes relies on stevia's property as a flavor enhancer-it sweetens and brings out the flavors of other foods. Numerous recipes in this book take advantage of the wonderful flavors and other qualities of fruit, which have then been greatly enlivened by using stevia. In some recipes one or two tablespoons of a mild natural sweetener, such as date sugar were added. The stevia picks up on this small amount of sweetener and magnifies it. **If you are unable to tolerate the sweeteners suggested in this book, than simply eliminate them from the recipes. The small amount suggested has a minimal effect on the overall quality of the baked goods. Note: it probably will not work to eliminate the sweetener in the chocolate recipes (see page 14 for further discussion).**

Stevia is stable at high temperatures well over the boiling point and in acidic foods. These properties make stevia easy to work with. For the cook this means there will be no concern about boiling stevia too long, baking at too high a temperature, or what the ingredients may be. Note: if you are steeping tea bags to derive sweetness and medicinal properties, there is no need to boil the herb. Keep the temperature below the boiling point lest it destroys other nutrients.

5

In addition to the sweet glycoside molecules found in stevia (primarily stevioside), there is also a bitter component. A direct correlation lies between bitterness and leaf quality. Environmental factors including soil, water, sunlight, air quality, farming practices, processing and storage can all influence the percent of sweet glycosides and other qualities in the leaf. The bitter taste is particularly evident in the powdered extracts. However, when appropriately diluted for consumption in a beverage or in baked goods, the bitter flavor disappears. **The amount of stevioside varies depending on source, though it is generally between 85 and 95%.**

The nutritional component of any food can be enhanced by the addition of dried stevia leaf. A powdered form can be added directly to foods or the liquid from an extracted tea may be used in place of other liquids in a recipe (see page 104 to make your own extract). There is a point, however, where the addition of powdered leaf will turn bakery green and an herb (or grassy) flavor may predominate. In general this happens after the addition of more than one tablespoon. This may not bother some. It works very well to use a combination of the herb or concentrate with an extract.

I have attempted in this volume and in Volume I to provide a broad range of dessert and beverage recipes. I have included many classic and popular recipes, which have been improved by using only fresh, whole, natural ingredients. In this volume, I also focused on reducing the fat content in many of the recipes and in developing a number of simple recipes for the busy cook.

Stevia is excellent for anyone who wishes to reduce the amount of sugars in their diet. If you wish to eliminate the extra calories sugar supplies and are concerned about the other negative health effects of sugar, stevia is the perfect choice Whether you just want to cut down on sugars or you can't have any sweeteners at all, the various stevia products can greatly assist you in your program. Enjoy exploring the uses of this wonderful herb in your daily life.

<u>Approximate Equivalents</u>

1/3 to 1/2 tsp. powdered extract	=	1 cup sugar
1/2 tsp. clear liquid extract	=	1 cup sugar
1-2 tbls. powdered leaf	=	1 cup sugar
2 tsp. green liquid conc.	=	1 cup brown sugar

HEALTH BENEFITS
OF *STEVIA*

The herb, *Stevia rebaudiana,* has been used for centuries by the Guarani Indians of Paraguay, who had several names for the plant, several of which are Kaa'-he-E, Caa'-ehe, or Ca-a-yupe- all referring to the sweet leaf or honey leaf. It is commonly known in South America as yerba dulce meaning sweet herb. The Guarani used stevia nutritionally and medicinally.

The plant came to the attention of the rest of the world when South American naturalist, Bertoni, "discovered" the plant in the late 1800's. After his report, the herb became widely used by herbalists in Paraguay.

Stevia's most obvious and notable characteristic is its sweet taste. However, the sweet taste is not due to carbohydrate-based molecules, but to several non-caloric molecules called glycosides. Individuals who cannot tolerate sugar or other sweeteners can use stevia. The first glycoside molecule was isolated from stevia in 1931 by two French chemists named Bridel and Lavieille and called stevioside.

During WW II, sugar shortages prompted England to begin investigation of stevia for use as a sweetener. Cultivation began under the direction of the Royal Botanical Gardens at Kew, but the project was abandoned in the aftermath of the war. Japan began cultivating stevia in hothouses in the 1950's. By the 1970's, Japan started using stevia commercially and today, they are the biggest users of the extract, which has captured 50% of Japan's sweetener industry.

Other aspects of stevia are capturing people's attention. The herb is sold in some South American countries to aid diabetics and hypoglycemics. Research has shown that a whole leaf concentrate has a regulating effect on the pancreas and helps stabilize blood sugar levels. Stevia is therefore useful to people with diabetes, hypoglycemia, and Candidiasis.

Other traditional uses of stevia are: lowers elevated blood pressure (hypertension), digestive aid that also reduces gas and stomach acidity, and for obesity. The herb acts as general tonic which increases energy levels and mental acuity.

Stevia has been shown to inhibit the growth and reproduction of bacteria that cause gum disease and tooth decay, making it an excellent addition to tooth pastes and mouthwashes. Many people have reported improvement in their oral health after adding stevia concentrate to their tooth paste and using it, diluted in water, as a daily mouthwash.

Stevia is useful in healing a number of skin problems. Whole stevia concentrates may be applied as a facial mask to soften and tighten the skin and smooth out wrinkles. Smooth the dark liquid over the entire face, allowing it to dry for at least 30-60 minutes. A drop of concentrate may be applied directly to any blemish, acne outbreak, lip or mouth sore. Stevia concentrate is also effective when used on seborrhea, dermatitis, and eczema. Reportedly, cuts and scratches heal more rapidly when stevia concentrate is applied.

Stevia concentrate added to soap eliminates dandruff and other scalp problems and improves the health and luster of the hair, also helping to retain natural hair color.

Refined sugar consumption continues to rise in the United States. According to the Center for Science in the Public Interest (Nov. 1998), sugar consumption rose by 25 pounds since 1986 to 152 pounds per person per year (calculated from sugar production figures). Sugar displaces nutritive calories leading to numerous health problems and obesity. A major factor contributing to this high rate is the widespread and continually growing habit of drinking sugar-laden soda pops.

This review of the therapeutic properties of stevia in no way constitutes an endorsement of such uses. Please consult a qualified physician before experimenting with this herb. At this time the FDA permits stevia to be sold only as a dietary supplement and in skin care products.

PRODUCTS AND USES

There are a number of stevia products on the market of two basic types: whole herb products and herbal extracts. Below are descriptions of available products. **Each product is preceded by a symbol. That symbol will also appear in the recipes as a reminder of what to use.**

⊕ STEVIA TEA BAGS

Drink stevia tea in convenient flow-thru bags by itself or blend with other herbs. Delicious hot or cold.

- Use stevia tea to replace the other liquids in a recipe.
- Stevia tea, alone or blended with other herbs or juice, may be frozen to make a flavorful and nutritious Popsicle.
- Stevia tea provides quick relief for upset stomach.
- After use, stevia tea bags may be dabbed on the face and eyes, or placed over the eyes for a few minutes to smooth and tighten the skin.
- Add stevia tea bags to any liquid that you want to sweeten.

⁂ POWDERED STEVIA LEAF

Finely ground dried stevia leaves may be used to enhance the flavor and nutritional value of many foods. It's about 10 to 30 times sweeter than sugar. Try these suggestions.

- Add to pizza, pasta sauce, sweet and sour sauce, and rice dishes.
- Add to salads, salad dressings, and potato salad.
- Sprinkle over steamed vegetables or baked potatoes.
- Use in soups, stews, and chili.
- Sprinkle over hot cereal. Mix with cinnamon in a shaker bottle to sprinkle on toast.
- Bake into breads and rolls.

✪STEVIA CONCENTRATE

Stevia leaves concentrated to a thick syrupy liquid by careful cooking in water. Stable for months. Flavor improves with age.

- Use in place of molasses or brown sugar in recipes such as molasses cookies, pumpkin pie, pumpkin bars, or spice cake.
- Apply as a facial mask to smooth and tighten the skin.
- Helps balance blood glucose and reduce cravings for sweets and fatty foods. Reduces hunger sensations.
- Inhibits the growth of bacteria that cause tooth decay and gum disease.

✱STEVIA POWDERED EXTRACT

A white-colored powder containing only the sweet glycoside molecules extracted from stevia leaves. A highly concentrated form generally 200 to 300 times sweeter than sugar. Does not adversely affect blood glucose.

- Useful in all baked goods including, pies, cakes, cookies, muffins.
- Excellent in beverages.
- Superb in puddings, gelatins, and frozen desserts.
- Enhances the flavors of fruit. Fruit salads come alive.

◈STEVIA CLEAR LIQUID EXTRACT

Contains a stevia powdered extract dissolved in a liquid base. It will not keep long without a preservative (commercial products generally contain one). Liquid extract is interchangeable with extract powder.

- Easy to use and convenient for carrying in your purse or for traveling.
- Excellent for beverages of all types including coffee, tea, home-made soda pop, and smoothies

NOTES: To take advantage of the full health benefits of stevia use the whole dried herb, or concentrate. One or two teaspoons of the concentrate and up to a tablespoon of the herb may be added to the muffins, cakes, cookies, and bars in the following recipes if desired.

If you don't care for the herb taste or green color in your products use the extract, either powdered or liquid. Often a combination of one of the herb products and an extract can be used with good success.

BAKING TIPS

PRE-HEAT OVEN - It can take up to 20 minutes to get an oven up to the right temperature.

PREPARATION - It is generally advised that all ingredients be brought to room temperature before mixing. I start warming everything up, including the room, by turning on the oven and taking everything out of the refrigerator before I begin. On the other hand, avoid over-warming eggs and butter in hot weather.

MEASURE ACCURATELY - All given measurements are "level", unless otherwise noted. "Scant" denotes slightly less than the full amount. "Heaping" means a rounded mound above level. To "pack" an ingredient press down on the substance until all the air is out.

VARIABLES - There are a number of variables in baking including the size of the eggs, moisture content of foods, bakeware, oven proficiency, measuring and mixing technique, temperature of ingredients, and weather. At times, I can't get cashew or soy whipped cream to bind (Volume I). It may be related to certain weather conditions.

PAN SIZE - Cake batter should fill the pan no less than half and no more than 2/3 full. If the pan is too large, the cake will not rise properly. If the pan is too small, the texture will be coarse and the batter may overflow or sink upon cooling. Loaf pans may be filled to 3/4 full. Fill muffin pans 3/4 full to full.

OVEN PLACEMENT - Place oven racks where you want them while oven is cold. The usual position is on a rack slightly above center. Try placing on a rack just below center for cakes and quick breads that are browning too fast. A single pan should be placed in the middle of the oven. Two pans on the same shelf should have 2 inches between them and between all four walls of the oven. If using two shelves, stagger the pans.

HIGH ALTITUDE BAKING - Adjustments to recipes may be required as altitude increases. Adjustments vary depending on whether baking cakes, cookies, etc. and how high the altitude is. Some of the changes include: under-beating the eggs, raising baking temperatures about 25°, and reducing the baking powder. See a standard cookbook for more details.

OVER MIXING of quick breads and muffins results in a coarse texture filled with holes and tunnels.

TESTING BAKING POWDER - Place 1 tsp. of powder in 1/3 cup hot water. Use if it bubbles effervescently.

MAKING BAKING POWDER - Single-acting: sift together

> *2 tsp. cream of tartar*
> *1 tsp. baking soda*
> *2 tsp. corn starch or arrowroot powder*

PIE CRUSTS - Roll out crust between two sheets of wax paper or use pastry cloth and rolling pin cover. Chilled pie dough may handle better. To prevent soggy bottom crust, brush with egg white or melted butter. Brush top with milk for a golden brown crust, with cold water for a flaky top crust.

REFRIGERATOR COOKIES - The trick is preventing the incorporation of too much flour when rolling out the dough. A rolling pin cover and pastry cloth helps.

BLANCHING ALMONDS - Boil 1 cup of water or enough to cover nuts. Pour the boiling water over nuts in a bowl. Let sit one minute. Drain and slip off the skins with thumb and index finger.

MAKING OAT FLOUR - Spread oat flakes on a cookie sheet. Toast in 300° oven for 15-20 minutes until golden brown. Grind in a blender to a fine flour.

MAKING SOUR MILK - Add 1 tbls. of fresh lemon juice or vinegar to 1 cup whole milk. Let stand for 10 minutes.

TOFU - Can be purchased fresh or in vacuum-packed cartons that have a long shelf life. Don't use old, sour-smelling tofu for uncooked blender drinks or puddings. Fresh tofu can be stored in the refrigerator for about one week if kept covered with water in a tightly covered container. Change the water everyday or so for greater freshness. Sour-smelling tofu may still be used for cooking. Either shave off the outer portions or boil the cake in water for about 20 minutes. Tofu is measured by weight in the following recipes.

EGGS – Yolks add richness, moistness, and tenderness to baked goods. The whites act as a leavening. Eggs also bind the ingredients together. Fresh eggs are best, though 1 or 2-day old eggs may not beat to a proper volume.

MILK – There are a number of milks commercially available other than dairy. In recipes calling for milk, use dairy, soy or rice milk. Oat milk is also available. These can be purchased fresh or in vacuum-packed cartons with a long shelf life. Also nut and seed milks can be made (see Volume I). Soy milk works very well in everything. Rice milk will not thicken with corn starch or arrowroot powder when making pudding.

FROZEN FRUIT - Frozen fruit, especially bananas, make blender drinks thick and creamy. To freeze bananas, peel first and place in air tight container or freezer bag. Bananas will turn brown after 10 to 14 days in the freezer.

RANCIDITY - Buy only fresh raw nuts and seeds. As with oils (except olive oil), store in the refrigerator. When fats spoil, they are said to be rancid. Oxygen, in the presence of heat and light, reacts with the unsaturated double bonds in the fat. This reaction produces peroxides; free-radicals that cause physiological damage. Oil, nuts, and whole grains, contain the natural antioxidants vitamin E and C. These are eventually used up in preventing fat decomposition. Rancid oils have a bitter taste. High frying temperatures of 400°F and above begin destroying unsaturated fatty acids. Smoking is a sign of the oil going bad.

13

CAROB– The pod of the tamarind tree is naturally sweet. This finely ground powder contains many minerals but no stimulants. Carob can be substituted in recipes calling for chocolate. Some recipes are improved by preparing a carob syrup first.

> **Directions for carob syrup:** In a small saucepan mix *1 cup of carob powder with 1 cup of water.* Cook over a low boil or 5-8 minutes stirring continually until smooth and creamy. If it is too thick add a little more water.

CHOCOLATE AND COCOA – Made from the hulled beans of an evergreen tree in the genus *Theobroma*. Part of the cocoa butter has been removed to make cocoa while cocoa butter is added to make baker's chocolate. Cocoa has significantly less calories.

> *3 tablespoons of cocoa = 1 square of baker's chocolate.*

I included chocolate recipes in the book because so many people love it. However, I was unable to offset the bitterness of cocoa or Baker's chocolate with stevia alone. I preferred using a little honey. Below is the ratio I found that worked well:

> *At least 2 tbls. of honey or equivalent with 1 square of Baker's chocolate or 3 tbls. of cocoa plus 1/2 to 3/4 teaspoons stevia extract.*

3 tbls. of honey would improve the flavor and texture even more. If you love chocolate and can eat a little sweetener, try these luscious recipes.

RICE FLOUR AND CORN MEAL - To eliminate grittiness, mix with the liquid in the recipe and heat to boiling while stirring.

CRANBERRIES – The tartness of these berries can be relieved by soaking the cranberries whole or chopped in stevia extract for several hours or overnight in the refrigerator.

SWEETENERS – There are two forms of sweeteners: granular and liquid. If you are able to eat some sweetener, then any listed below may be used interchangeably. Some people can tolerate one type better than another. I found that the addition of even a tiny amount of sweetener improves the flavor of the product and makes it more satisfying, especially when no fruit is called for. I use it like a condiment. **If you cannot tolerate sweeteners then don't add it to the recipe.**

If the recipe calls for a granular sweetener use:
> date sugar
> granular Fruitsource
> raw sugar OR
> brown sugar

If the recipe call for a liquid sweetener use:
> honey
> maple syrup
> liquid Fruitsource
> rice syrup OR
> barley malt

STORING SPICES AND HERBS – Buy dried spices and herbs as fresh as possible. Health food stores and herb shops are good places to buy. Store spices and herbs in covered glass containers in a dry closed cupboard.

STORING BAKED GOODS - For longer-lasting freshness, store bakery made with whole foods in the refrigerator if not eaten right away. It is my observation that the sweetness of stevia baked goods seem to improve in time. After they have cooled or have even been refrigerated for a day or two (or frozen), the sweet flavors seem more developed. You can bring back the freshness of a refrigerated or frozen baked item by placing it in the microwave oven for about 20 seconds (about 30 seconds if frozen).

THICKENERS – There are a number of thickening agents available. There are two basic types, starches or gelatins.

Starches

•Corn starch: A refined powder processed from the endosperm of the corn kernel. Used to thicken puddings and sauces. Care is necessary in preventing both the undercooking and overcooking of the starch.

•Arrowroot powder: The beaten pulp of the tuberous rootstocks of the tropical American maranta plant. Thickens sauces, puddings, and glazes after several minutes of cooking on low heat. It thickens quickly with little trouble but the texture is not as smooth and creamy as with cornstarch.

•Tapioca: Milled from the dried starch of the cassava root. Must be brought to the boiling point then removed from the heat. Tapioca thickens as it cools. Used for sauces, puddings, and glazes. Often used to thicken fruit pies.

•Kudzu (or kuzu) root: A powder made from a vine that originally was grown in the Far East, but now is a widespread invasive throughout the southeastern U.S. Dissolve in a small amount of liquid, then added to other simmering liquids. Kudzu thickens without boiling. Used for sauces, puddings, and glazes.

•Potato starch: Made from cooked potatoes that have been dried and ground. Generally used in soups and gravies.

•Wheat flour: May be used to thicken sauces and puddings. Twice the amount must be used as compared to the other thickeners above. May use in combination with the others.

Gelatins

•Agar-agar: Also known as kanten. Boiled and dried seaweed. *Use 1 tablespoon to 1 cup of liquid.* Place agar in the liquid, bring to a boil. Reduce heat and simmer about 5 minutes until agar is dissolved. Thickens to a clear gel upon cooling.

•Gelatin: An animal by-product. Generally *use 1 tablespoon for every 2 cups of liquid.* Sprinkle gelatin over a portion of the cold liquid and let it soak for 3-5 minutes. Simmer the liquid until the gelatin is dissolved and add it to the rest of the liquid.

•Kosher gelatin: contains carageenan, locust bean gum, and malto-dextrin.

SUBSTITUTIONS

1 tsp. baking powder	=	1/2 tsp. baking soda + 1 tsp. cream of tartar
	or	1/2 tsp. baking soda + 1/2 c. buttermilk or yogurt
	or	1/2 tsp. baking soda + 1/2 cup molasses or honey
1 tsp. baking soda	=	1/2 tsp baking soda + 1 1/2 tsp. lemon juice

1 cup buttermilk	=	1 cup cashew milk + 1 tbls. lemon juice
	or	1 cup yogurt
	or	1 cup sour milk
	or	4 oz tofu + 1/2 c. soy milk + 1 tbls. lemon juice

Note: cashew milk is not a cultured product.

1 tbls. corn starch	=	1 tbls. arrowroot powder
	or	2 tbls. wheat flour
	or	1 tbls. potato flour

1 egg (as a binder)	=	1/4 c. cashew or almond butter or tahini
	or	2 oz. tofu
	or	1/2 ripe banana
	or	packaged powdered egg replacer
	or	1/4 cup apple butter

1 tbls. gelatin	=	2 tbls. agar flakes

BEVERAGES

ORANGE POP

A cool, light and refreshing thirst-quencher

2 cups fresh-squeezed orange juice (strained)
1 1/2 cups purified water
30-40 drops clear liquid stevia extract ◈ OR
1/2 tsp. powdered extract (to taste) ✻
8-12 ounces carbonated water (flavored or unflavored)

Squeeze the oranges (about 6-8 oranges) and strain out the pulp. Mix in the water and the stevia extract. Chill covered in the refrigerator.

Add the carbonated water to each glass just before serving. Best if used in 1-2 days.

Serves: 4

NOTE: If you don't have carbonated water, use another cup of regular water to make an orangeade. It's pleasant.

ROOT BEER

3 tbls. sarsaparilla root (about 1/2 ounce)
1 tbls. licorice root
1 qt. purified water
2-3 tsp. dried stevia leaf 🌿 *OR*
3-4 stevia teabags ⊞
2 qts. carbonated water
stevia extract to taste (powdered or liquid ✳ ◈)

Simmer the sarsaparilla and licorice root in the quart of water for about 45 minutes. **Do not boil-it brings out bitter principles.** Add the stevia tea bags and simmer for 15 minutes longer.

Strain the plant material and return the pan to the burner. Simmer on very low until liquid is reduced to half. Remove from heat and strain through a cheesecloth. Will be left with about 12 ounces of concentrate. Chill in the refrigerate.

Before serving add a quart of carbonated water. Two ounces of concentrate to 10-12 ounces of carbonated water. Add stevia extract to taste if more sweetener is desired.

Serves: 6 large glasses

SUGGESTION: May use 2 tbls. of sarsaparilla and 2 tbls licorice root OR add any other barks or herbs of your choice.

QUICK CRANBERRY PUNCH

Sparkling fresh and alive-sure to jazz up any party

12 ounces frozen unsweetened cran-apple juice
concentrate (thawed)
2 quarts carbonated water (flavored or unflavored)
40 –50 drops of liquid stevia extract (about 3/4 tsp.) ◈
***OR** 1/2 to 3/4 tsp. powdered extract* ✻
slices of oranges and lemons (optional)

Place the unthawed juice, carbonated water and stevia in a large punch bowl or pitcher just before serving. Serve with round slices of oranges and/or lemons floating on the surface if desired.

Serves: 8

VARIATION: Also excellent with a raspberry juice blend concentrate.

MANGO PAPAYA SMOOTHIE

A sweet and creamy treat from India

1 quart mango or papaya juice or a blend
1 cup plain low-fat yogurt
1/2 tsp. powdered stevia extract ✱

Mix ingredients together in a blender until smooth.

Serves: 4 (large glasses)

NOTE: This is an excellent beverage following a hot spicy meal, especially Indian food.

CREAMY DATE SHAKE

Wonderfully thick and creamy-a real delight

4 dates (pitted and chopped)
8 ounces milk
1 lb. soft or silken tofu
4 frozen bananas (small to medium)
2 tsp. vanilla
1 tsp. powdered stevia extract ✽

Grind the chopped dates and milk together until the dates are well ground. Add the rest of the ingredients and blend until creamy. Use the pulse button at first, keeping the sides scraped down. May use a food processor.

Serves: 4 (large glasses)

HOT COCOA

Rich and chocolaty-like Mom used to make

3 tbls. cocoa
1/2 tsp. powdered stevia extract ✳
4-5 cups milk
2 tbls. honey or maple syrup
1 tsp. vanilla extract

Mix the cocoa and stevia together in a medium-sized sauce pan. Add about 1/4 cup milk to the dry ingredients to make a paste. Thin the paste with about 1/2 cup of milk. Add the honey or maple syrup while bringing to a low boil. Boil for 2-3 minutes. Add rest of milk to desired richness. Add vanilla and return to burner until heated through.

Serves: 4-5

NOTE: Be careful not to scorch the cocoa. Use a heavy-bottomed pan and watch closely.

VARIATION: May add a tsp. of cinnamon and a pinch of nutmeg.

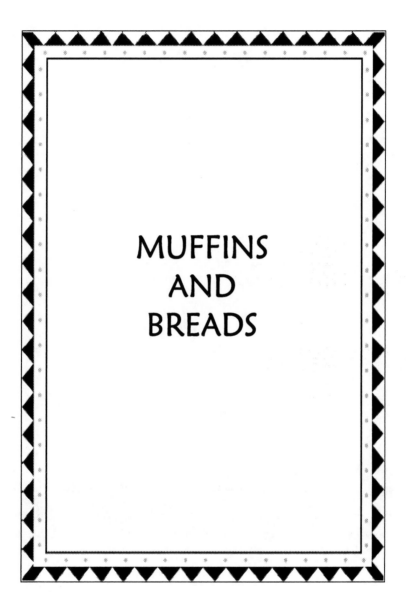

MUFFINS
AND
BREADS

YAM PECAN MUFFINS

1 cup cooked yams (packed)
2 eggs
6 tbls. oil
2 tbls. date sugar
1/3 tsp. powdered stevia extract ✳
3/4 tsp. stevia concentrate ✪
1/2 tsp. maple flavoring
1 tbls. lemon juice
1 cup milk

1 1/2 cups w.w. pastry flour
1 cup unbleached flour
3 tbls. soy flour
1 tsp. baking soda
1/2 tsp. baking powder
1 tsp. cinnamon
1/2 tsp. nutmeg
1/4 tsp. salt
3/4 cup chopped pecans

Preheat oven to 375°. Oil muffin tins. Yield: 12 muffins

Cook yams by peeling, cutting, and steaming. Put aside to cool.

In a mixing bowl, beat the eggs into the oil with a wire wisk. Beat in the date sugar, stevia extract, concentrate, and maple flavoring.

In a cup, mix lemon juice and milk. Set aside. While milk is fermenting sift dry ingredients together and chop the pecans. Beat the soured milk into the egg mixture. Stir in the yams. Break up any large pieces of yam but leave the batter a bit lumpy.

Fold in the dry ingredients. Add the pecans just before the flour is completely mixed in (may save a small portion of the pecans to sprinkle on the top-lightly press in). Spoon into oiled muffin pans. **Bake 25-30 minutes**. Remove from pan and cool on a rack.

CRANBERRY ORANGE MUFFINS

1 cup fresh cranberries (chopped)
1 tsp. powdered stevia extract ✳
1/3 cup oil
2 tbls. tahini
2 eggs
1 cup orange juice (fresh or frozen)
1/4 cup yogurt
1-2 tbls. honey or maple syrup
1 tsp. vanilla extract
grated rind of 1 orange

2 1/2 cups w. w. pastry flour
2 tbls. soy flour
1 tsp. baking soda
1/2 tsp. baking powder
1/4 tsp. salt

Preheat oven to 375°. Oil muffin pans. Yield: 12 muffins

Chop the cranberries by pulsing on grind in the blender a few times. Mix the stevia into the cranberries in a small bowl. Set aside.

In a large mixing bowl, beat the oil, tahini, and eggs together with a wire wisk. Mix the orange juice and yogurt together in a cup, then add to the egg mixture. Wisk in the honey (or maple syrup), vanilla, and orange rind.

Sift the dry ingredients together. Fold the dry ingredients into the wet stirring as little as possible. Mix cranberries into batter just before flour is completely mixed in. Spoon into muffin pans. **Bake 25-30 minutes**. Remove from pan and cool on a rack.

SUGGESTION: Soak the cranberries in the stevia overnight in the refrigerator if possible.

PEANUT BUTTER BANANA CHOCOLATE CHIP MUFFINS

3 tbls. oil
1/3 cup chunky natural peanut butter
1 egg
2 ripe bananas (small)
1/2 cup unsweetened fruit juice
1 tsp. vanilla extract
1/3 tsp. powdered stevia extract ✱
1/2 cup yogurt or buttermilk

1 3/4 cups w.w. pastry flour
1/4 cup soy flour
1/2 tsp. baking soda
1/2 tsp. baking powder
1/4 tsp. salt (only if peanut butter is unsalted)
1/3 cup chips (chocolate or carob)

Preheat oven to 375°. Oil muffin pans. Yield: 10-12 muffins.

In a large mixing bowl, mix the oil and peanut butter together. Beat in the egg.

Blend one banana and the fruit juice together in a blender with the vanilla and stevia extract. Mix into the batter.

Mash the other banana in a bowl and gently stir into batter. Fold in the yogurt (or buttermilk).

Sift the dry ingredients together. Fold the dry ingredients into the wet stirring as little as possible. Mix the chips in just before flour is completely blended. Spoon into muffin pans. **Bake 25-30 minutes**. Remove from the pan and cool on a rack.

CARROT MUFFINS

1 cup grated carrots
3/4 cup pineapple juice or pineapple blend
1/2 tsp. powdered stevia extract ✳
1/2 tsp. stevia concentrate ✪
1/3 cup oil
1 egg
1/2 cup applesauce
1 tsp. vanilla

2 1/4 cups w.w. pastry flour
3/4 tsp. baking soda
1 tsp. baking powder
1/8 tsp. salt
3/4 tsp. cinnamon
1/4 tsp. nutmeg
1/4 cup chopped walnuts or sunflower seeds
1/4 cup raisins (optional)

Preheat oven to 375°. Oil muffin pans. Yield: 12 muffins.

Grate the carrots into a small bowl. Add the juice, stevia extract and concentrate. Set aside to soak.

In a large mixing bowl, beat the oil, egg, applesauce, and vanilla together.

Sift the dry ingredients together in a separate bowl.

Add the carrots to the wet ingredients. Fold the dry ingredients into the wet. Add the nuts and raisins just before flour is completely mixed.

Spoon into muffins pan. **Bake for 30 minutes**. Remove from pans and cool on a rack.

ZUCCHINI MUFFINS

1 cup grated zucchini (loosely packed, then pressed)
1/3 cup oil
1 egg
1/2 cup unsweetened applesauce
1/2 cup plain yogurt OR buttermilk
1/3 tsp. powdered stevia extract ✳
1/2 tsp. stevia concentrate ✪
1 tbls. date sugar
1 tsp. vanilla extract

1 3/4 cups w.w. pastry flour
1/4 cup soy flour
1/4 tsp. salt
1 tsp. baking soda
1 tsp. baking powder
1 tsp. powdered stevia herb 🌿
1 tsp. cinnamon
1/2 tsp. nutmeg
1/4 cup chopped walnuts or sunflower seeds (optional)

Preheat oven to 375°. Oil the muffin pans. Yield: 12 muffins.

Grate the zucchini and measure - lightly packing the cup. After measuring, squeeze the water out of the zucchini by using a cheese-cloth or squeeze using your palm by making a fist. Set aside.

In a mixing bowl beat the oil and egg together with a wire wisk. Add the applesauce, yogurt (or buttermilk), stevia extract, stevia concentrate, date sugar, and vanilla and mix well.

Sift the flours, salt, leavenings, stevia herb, and spices together. Fold the dry ingredients into the wet, stirring quickly. Add the nuts or sunflowers seeds just before the batter is completely blended. Spoon into muffin pans.

Bake 25-30 minutes. Remove from pans and cool on a rack.

DATE NUT BREAD

1/3 cup oil
2 eggs
3/4 cup applesauce
1/4 cup plain yogurt
1/2 tsp. powdered stevia extract ✳
1/2 tsp. stevia concentrate ✪
1 tsp. vanilla

2 1/4 cups w.w. pastry flour
1 tsp. baking powder
1/4 tsp. salt
3-4 chopped dates
1/2 cup chopped walnuts

Preheat oven to 350°. Butter a medium-sized loaf pan.

Beat the oil and eggs together in a large mixing bowl. Mix in the applesauce, yogurt, stevia extract, stevia concentrate, and vanilla.

Stir the flour, baking soda, and salt together. Mix the dry ingredients into the wet, stirring just enough to mix. Add the dates and the nuts just before flour is completely mixed in.

Spoon the batter into the loaf pan. **Bake 50 to 60 minutes**.

31

YAM DROP BISCUITS

1/2 cup cooked yam (packed)
1 1/2 cups whole wheat pastry flour
1/4 tsp. salt
1/4 tsp. powdered stevia extract ✱ *AND/OR*
1 tsp. powdered stevia leaf ༀ
3 tbls. butter or margarine
1/2 cup milk

Preheat oven to 400°. Yield: 16 biscuits.

Cook the yam by peeling, cutting into pieces, and steaming.

Sift the flour, salt, and stevia together into a large mixing bowl. Cut the butter (or margarine) into the flour with a pastry blender or fork until it is evenly distributed.

Blend the milk and yam together in the blender. Make a well in the center of the flour. Pour the liquid into the flour and mix. Batter should pull away from the sides of the bowl. Add a little more flour if necessary.

Drop from a spoon onto an unoiled cookie sheet. **Bake 12-15 minutes**.

NOTE: May use 3 tbls. of oil instead of butter or margarine but the flavor and texture will not be as good. Also be careful about adding too much flour.

 # BREAKFAST SWEET ROLLS

BREAD MACHINE DOUGH

1 cup water
1 egg
3 tbls. oil
1 1/2 tbls. honey*
1/2 tsp. salt
1 tbls. powdered stevia leaf 🌿
3 cups w.w. bread flour
1 pkg. dry yeast

Add the ingredients to the bread machine pan in order listed. Mix the stevia leaf into the flour before adding. Set the machine to the Dough Cycle and start machine.

Remove dough to lightly floured board. Roll out to about 1/4-inch thick in a rectangle approximately 10 x 18-inches.

*A small amount of sugar is necessary for the yeast to live and grow.

FILLING

1 cup coarsely ground walnuts
1/2 tsp. powdered stevia extract ✳
1/2 tsp. stevia concentrate ✪
1 tsp. cinnamon
6 dates
2/3 cup water
1 tsp. vanilla

While dough is in machine prepare filling. Chop walnuts and mix in a small bowl with stevia extract, stevia concentrate, and cinnamon. Set aside.

Preheat oven to 350°.

(over)

Cut up dates and place in a small pan. Cover with water and cook until a creamy paste. Spread paste over rolled out dough. Sprinkle nut mixture evenly over date paste.

Start at one long edge and roll up dough. Cut into 1-inch sections. Place on buttered cookie sheet. Flatten with palm. Cover with a cloth and let rise in a warm location for 45 minutes -1 hour.

Bake 25-30 minutes. Butter tops upon removal from oven.

CAKES

MAPLE TOFU CHEESECAKE

CRUST

1 1/2 cups ginger snaps or graham crackers
(finely ground)
5-6 tbls. butter or margarine (melted)

Place the cookies or crackers in a plastic bag, close the bag and crush with a rolling pin. Place in a small bowl.

Mix the melted butter into the crumbs until well blended. Press the crumbs into the bottom and 2 inches up the sides of a 9-inch spring-release pan. The crust may be baked in a 300° oven or left unbaked. If used unbaked, the crust must be thoroughly chilled before filling.

FILLING

2 lbs. medium to firm tofu (drained)
1/2 cup oil
3/4 tsp. powdered stevia extract ✳
4 tbls. maple syrup
2 tbls. apple butter
1/2 tsp. maple flavoring
1 tsp. vanilla extract
1/8 tsp. salt

Bring oven up to 325°.

Drain tofu sections on paper towels. Hasten process by placing a plate on top for about 15 minutes.

Process all the ingredients together in a blender or food processor until creamy. If using a blender, it will have to be done in two batches. Use the pulse button until it is smooth enough to blend.

Spoon filling into the pan. Place a tray or cookie sheet on lower rack beneath the pan (for leakage). **Bake 45 minutes**. Turn off oven but leave pan in oven 1/2 hour longer. Cool on the counter then refrigerate one to several days.

CHOCOLATE CHEESECAKE

CRUST

See crust recipe page 36.

FILLING

4 squares Baker's chocolate
4 cups low-fat cottage cheese
2 tbls. butter (melted)
4 eggs
6-8 tbls. honey or maple syrup
1 tsp. powdered stevia extract ✻
1 tsp. vanilla extract
1/4 tsp. salt
1/4 cup flour

Melt the Baker's chocolate over low heat in a small pan. Add the butter and melt.

Press the cottage cheese through a fine sieve (strainer). Place in a mixing bowl. Add the melted chocolate and butter.

Beat the eggs in a small bowl. Add eggs in 4 parts to the cottage cheese, beating well after each addition. Mix in the honey (or maple syrup), stevia, vanilla, salt, and flour. Stir until mixture is smooth and thoroughly blended.

Pour gently into cake pan. Bake in 300° oven for 1 hour. Shut oven off but leave cake inside for 1 1/2 hours longer. Do not open oven door.

Cool on the counter then chill the cake in the refrigerator before serving. Up to 12 hours or more is recommended.

SPICE CAKE

1/3 cup oil
2 eggs
1/2 cup unsweetened applesauce
1/4 cup yogurt
1/4 cup milk
1 1/2 tsp. stevia concentrate ✪
1 tbls. date sugar or granular Fruitsource

3/4 cup w.w. pastry flour
1 cup unbleached white flour
1/2 tsp. baking soda
1 tsp. baking powder
1/4 tsp. salt
1 tsp. cinnamon
1/4 tsp. nutmeg
1/4 tsp. allspice

Preheat oven to 350°. Oil an 8-inch square or round pan.

Whip the oil and eggs together in a mixing bowl. Stir in the applesauce. Thin the yogurt with the milk and add. Mix in the stevia concentrate, date sugar (or Fruitsource).

Sift the flours, leavenings, and spices together. Stir the dry ingredients into the wet until they are well blended.

Spoon batter into pan. Smooth the top surface with a spatula and **bake for 40 minutes**.

Top with a lemon icing or whipped cream topping (see Volume I).

BANANA CAKE

1/4 cup oil
2 eggs
1/3 cup plain low-fat yogurt
1 large ripe banana (mashed)
1/2 tsp. powdered stevia extract ✱
1/2 tsp. vanilla

1 cup w.w. pastry flour (scant)
1/2 cup unbleached white flour
1/2 tsp. baking soda
1 tsp. baking powder
pinch of salt

Preheat oven to 350°. Oil an 8-inch square or round pan.

Beat the oil and eggs together in a mixing bowl. Mix in the yogurt, mashed banana, stevia, and vanilla.

Sift together the flours, leavenings, and salt. Add to liquid mixture and beat just until smooth.

Spoon batter into the pan. Smooth the top surface with a spatula. **Bake for 30 minutes**.

SERVING SUGGESTION: Serve topped with fresh, sliced, stevia-sweetened strawberries and a whipped topping.

DUTCH APPLE CAKE

TOPPING

2 cups chopped apples (about 2 large apples)
1/2 cup chopped almonds or walnuts
2 dates
3/4 tsp. cinnamon
1/4 tsp. nutmeg
1/2 tsp. almond or vanilla extract
pinch of salt
1/3 tsp. powdered stevia extract ✳
1/2 tsp. stevia concentrate ✪
1 tbls. lemon juice

Preheat oven to 350°. Butter a medium-sized casserole dish or glass baking pan (about 8-inch size).

Chop the apples into thin pieces. Place in a mixing bowl. Chop the nuts and dates; mix with the apples. Stir all the rest of the topping ingredients into the apples. Place in the bottom of the baking pan.

CAKE

2 cups w.w. pastry flour
1 tsp. baking soda
1/4 tsp. salt
1/2 tsp. powdered stevia extract ✳
1/4 cup butter
1 egg
1 cup buttermilk

Stir the flour, baking soda, salt, and stevia together in a bowl. Cut the butter into the flour and mix until well distributed. Beat the egg and buttermilk together lightly and stir into flour mix. Stir just until mixed. Batter will be stiff.

Spoon batter over apples. **Bake 40-45 minutes**. Upon removal from the oven, loosen the sides of the cake and turn over onto a plate immediately.

CAROB PECAN CAKE

1/2 cup butter (softened)
2 tbls. date sugar
3/4 tsp. powdered stevia extract *
3/4 cup carob powder
3 eggs
1/2 cup milk
1/2 cup yogurt
1/2 cup unsweetened applesauce
1 1/2 tsp. vanilla extract
2 cups w.w. pastry flour
1 tsp. baking soda
1 1/2 tsp. baking powder
1/4 tsp. salt

Preheat oven to 350°. Butter two 8-inch round cake pans.

Soften and cream the butter in a mixing bowl. Cream in the date sugar, stevia and about 1/4 cup of the carob powder. Beat in the eggs with a hand mixer. Add the rest of the carob and beat. Mix in the milk, yogurt, applesauce, and vanilla.

Sift the dry ingredients together. Add the dry ingredients to the wet, mixing just until well blended. Spoon into pans and smooth the top surface. **Bake 22-25 minutes**. Cool on a rack, then turn out cakes.

FROSTING

8-10 dates
1/3 to 1/2 cup unsweetened fruit juice
2/3 cup carob powder
2/3 cup water
1/3 tsp. powdered stevia extract *
1 tsp. vanilla extract
2 tbls. butter
1/2 cup chopped pecans

(over)

In a small sauce pan cook the chopped dates in the fruit juice, stirring occasionally until smooth and creamy. Set aside.

In another small pan cook the carob powder and water at a low-boil for 5-8 minutes. Beat in the butter, stevia, and vanilla. Add the cooked dates and beat until well blended.

Chop the pecans.

Spread some of the frosting between the cake layers. Spread the rest of the frosting on the top and sides of the cake. Sprinkle the nuts on the top.

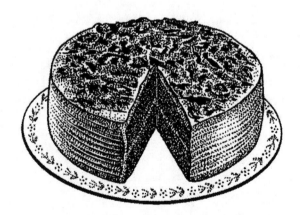

CUSTARDS
AND
CREPES

BANANA COCONUT CUSTARD

Light and delicate in flavor and texture

1 1/2 cups milk (dairy or soy)
1 large ripe banana
2 eggs
1/4 cup unsweetened coconut
1 tsp. vanilla extract
1/2 tsp. powdered stevia extract *
sprinkle of nutmeg

Preheat oven to 325°. Have ready 4 individual custard cups and a baking dish filled to 1 inch deep with water.

Blend all the ingredients together in a blender on low. If frothy, pour mixture through a strainer before pouring into the dishes.

Place custard cups in water bath. **Bake 45-50 minutes** until a knife inserted near the side of the dish comes out clean. Remove from oven and chill on a rack. Serve or refrigerate.

FLAN

4 eggs (fresh)
2 cups milk
1 tsp. vanilla
3/4 tsp. powdered stevia extract ✱
1 tbls. flour
pinch of salt
2 tbls. liquid Fruitsource or rice syrup

Preheat oven to 315-325°. Have ready an 8-inch shallow, straight-sided pan.

Place the eggs, milk, vanilla, stevia, flour, and salt in a blender. Process on low for several minutes. Set aside. If frothy, pour mixture through a strainer before pouring into the baking dish.

Heat the Fruitsource (or rice syrup) in a small sauce pan to a rolling boil. Spoon Fruitsource into bottom of baking dish and quickly roll around to coat the bottom and sides.

After the caramel glaze has cooled and hardened, pour in the custard. Place baking dish in a water bath by filling a larger sized pan with 1 inch of water. The water in the bath must not boil. If 325° is too hot reduce temperature to 315°.

Bake approximately 2 hours. Check for doneness by inserting a knife part-way in near sides of dish. If the knife comes out clean, custard is done.

Cool on rack 1 hour. Turn out onto a plate. Loosen sides of custard if necessary. Refrigerate several hours before serving.

 # CREPES

2 eggs
1 cup milk
1 cup w.w. pastry flour (scant)
2 tsp. oil
dash of salt
pinch of powdered stevia extract ✳

Blend all ingredients together in a blender on low. Set covered in the blender 20 to 30 minutes.

Pour approximately 1/4 cup of batter at a time into a small, heated, oiled, heavy-bottomed frying pan. Tilt pan until batter reaches all sides. When the bottom is lightly browned, flip crepe and lightly brown the other side.

Yield: 8 crepes

Serve filled with Apple or Pear Filling (page 83) or
Plum Sauce (page 79) and rolled up.

SIMPLY FRUIT

BAKED PEARS

A simple way to enjoy this seasonal fruit

10-12 pears
1 cup fruit juice
1 tbls. corn starch or arrowroot powder
2 tbls. lemon juice
1 tsp. cinnamon
1/2 tsp. powdered stevia extract *

Preheat oven to 350°.

Peel, core and quarter the pears. Place 8 to 10 of the quartered pears in a large baking dish (approximately 9 x 13 inches).

Place several of the pears in a blender with the rest of the ingredients. Blend until smooth. Pour mixture over pears in baking dish.

Bake covered about 1 hour until pears are tender. Pears vary greatly in hardness and some types may take quite long to soften.

SUMMER FRUIT SALAD

Stevia really makes a fruit salad come alive! Use the fruit suggested below or your favorite combination.

2 cups melon chunks or balls (about 1/2 melon)
1 cup blueberries (or other fresh berries)
2 large bananas (sliced)
2 ripe peaches or nectarines
1 cup cherries or grapes (halved)

Cut up the fruit and place in a large bowl. Dress with one of the following dressings and chill in the refrigerator before serving.

Serves: 6-8

DRESSING 1

1/4 cup frozen unsweetened orange juice concentrate OR orange blend (thawed)
1 tbls. lemon juice
1/2 tsp. powdered stevia extract ✽

DRESSING 2

1 cup yogurt
1 tsp. vanilla extract
1/2 tsp. powdered stevia extract ✽

FRUIT COMPOTE

1 tbls. mulling spices OR 1 tsp. whole cloves, 1 tsp.
whole allspice, and one cinnamon stick
2-3 stevia tea bags ⊞
1 1/2 cups water
2 cups of fresh fruit of choice (diced or halved if using
grapes and/or cherries).

Simmer the spices and stevia bags in the water for about 10-15 minutes. Remove spices and stevia. Return to heat and bring to a boil. Drop the fruit into the liquid. Immediately reduce to a simmer. Simmer about 1 minute or until fruit is tender. Serve immediately in the sweet, spicy sauce.

If using very soft fruit like ripe peaches or ripe pears, you may need to quickly cool the fruit down by placing pan in a cold water bath to keep the fruit from overcooking. If using hard fruit like apples, they will have to be cooked longer than the other fruit.

Suggested fruit: pears, peaches, kiwi, cherries, grapes, blueberries.

Serves: 4

COOKIES
AND
BARS

COCONUT FIG CHEWS

1/2 cup chopped figs (10-12)
1/2 cup unsweetened fruit juice or water
1 cup unsweetened coconut
1/2 cup ground sesame seeds
1/8 tsp. salt
1/2 tsp. powdered stevia extract ✳
2 tbls. cashew butter
1/3 cup w.w. pastry flour

Preheat oven to 350°. Oil a cookie sheet. Yield: 12-14 cookies.

Stew the chopped figs in the fruit juice or water for 8-10 minutes. Add the coconut to the pan, mix, and set aside.

Grind the sesame seeds in a blender. In a mixing bowl place the stewed figs and coconut, sesame seeds, salt, stevia, cashew butter, and flour. Mix well. Shape the cookies with your hands. Place on cookie sheet and flatten slightly.

Bake 12-14 minutes.

NOTE: May add one tsp. of powdered stevia herb. ❧

JAM DOT COOKIES

1/3 cup oil
1 egg
2 tbls. apple butter
3 tbls. plain yogurt
2 tbls. granular Fruitsource or date sugar
1/2 tsp. powdered stevia extract ✳
1 tsp. vanilla

1 1/2 cups w.w. pastry flour
1/4 tsp. baking soda
1/8 tsp. salt
about 1/2 cup jam or other filling

In a mixing bowl whip the oil and egg together. Mix in the apple butter, yogurt, Fruitsource (or date sugar), vanilla, and stevia.

Stir the flour, baking soda, and salt together. Mix dry ingredients into wet. Batter should start to pull away from the sides.

Refrigerate dough for at least 2 hours.

Preheat oven to 325°. Butter a cookie sheet. Remove batter from refrigerator. Form cookies into 1-inch balls and place on the cookie sheet. Flatten balls slightly with palm. Make a depression in the center of the cookies (the tip of a honey dipper works great-dip it in flour to keep it from sticking). Spoon some jam or other filling into the depression.

Bake 15-20 minutes. Yield: about 20 cookies.

PECAN SANDIES

6 tbls. softened butter or margarine
2 tbls. tahini
2 tbls. date sugar or granular Fruitsource
1/2 tsp. powdered stevia extract *
1 tsp. vanilla
2 eggs (lightly beaten)
2 tbls. milk

1/2 cup coarsely ground pecans
1/3 cup chopped pecans
15 pecan halves
1 1/4 cups w.w. pastry flour
1/4 tsp. salt
1/2 tsp. baking powder

Mix the softened butter (or margarine) with the tahini, date sugar (or Fruitsource), stevia extract, and vanilla in a mixing bowl. Add the beaten eggs.

Sift the flour, salt, and baking powder together. Mix the flour, ground pecans, and chopped pecans into the batter. The batter should pull away from the sides of the bowl. If the batter is too sticky add 1 or 2 tablespoons more flour. Be careful about adding too much flour.

Refrigerate batter for several hours or more.

Preheat oven to 350°. Oil a cookie sheet. Yield: 18 cookies.

Shape the dough into balls with your hands. Flatten the balls with your palm on the cookie sheet. Press a pecan half in the center of each cookie. **Bake for 15 minutes**.

MOLASSES COOKIES

1/4 cup oil
2 tbls. tahini or cashew butter
1/4 cup apple butter
3/4 tsp. stevia concentrate ✪
1 1/2 tbls. Blackstrap molasses
1 tsp. vanilla extract

1 cup w.w. pastry flour
1/4 tsp. baking soda
1/4 tsp. salt
1/2 tsp. cinnamon
1/4 tsp. ginger
1/8 tsp. cloves

Preheat oven to 350°. Oil a cookie sheet. Yield: 12 cookies.

Mix the oil and tahini (or cashew butter) together in a mixing bowl. Add the apple butter, stevia concentrate, molasses, and vanilla. Mix well.

Mix the flour, leavening, salt, and spices together. Add the dry ingredients to the wet.

Roll into balls and place on cookie sheet. Flatten with the palm of your hand. **Bake for 15 minutes**.

NOTE: May use 1/2 tsp. stevia extract and 2 tbls. molasses. If you don't want to use the molasses, use a total of 1 tsp. of stevia concentrate and 1 extra tbls. of apple butter.

CHOCOLATE CHIP COOKIES

Reduced Fat-Vegan

1/2 cup cashew butter
1/4 cup oil
1/2 cup apple butter
1/3 tsp. powdered stevia extract ✳
1/2 tsp. stevia concentrate ✪
1 tsp. vanilla extract
1 cup w.w. pastry flour
1/4 tsp. baking soda
1/4 tsp. salt
1/2 cup chocolate chips OR carob chips

Preheat oven to 375°. Oil a cookie sheet. Yield: 16 cookies.

Cream the cashew butter and oil together in a mixing bowl. Add the apple butter, stevia extract, concentrate, and vanilla

Stir the flour, baking soda, and salt together. Add the dry ingredients to the wet. Stir in the chocolate chips.

Spoon onto cookie sheet.
Flatten with palm of the hand.
Bake 12-15 minutes.

DATE BARS

CRUST & TOPPING

3/4 cup rolled oats
1 cup w.w. pastry flour
1/4 cup unsweetened coconut
1/4 tsp. powdered stevia extract ✱
1/8 tsp. salt
6 tbls. oil
1-2 tbls. maple syrup

Preheat oven to 350°. Oil a 8-inch square or 5 x 9-inch pan.

Mix the oats, flour, coconut, stevia, and salt together in a mixing bowl. Stir the oil into the dry ingredients. Rub the maple syrup in with your fingers.

Press about 2/3rds of the mixture firmly into bottom of baking pan. Use the rest for the topping.

FILLING

1 1/2 cups chopped dates (not packed)
about 2/3 cup water
pinch of salt
1/3 tsp. powdered stevia extract ✱

Place all the ingredients in a small sauce pan and cook over low heat until creamy. Add a little more water if necessary. (Should be a thick, creamy spreadable paste.)

Spread the date filling over the crust. Sprinkle the topping over the filling. Press the topping lightly into the filling with a fork.

Bake 30 minutes. Cool thoroughly before cutting.

SESAME CRISPS

3-4 tbls. oil
3/4 cup cashew or almond butter
1/2 cup apple butter
2 tbls. maple syrup
1/2 tsp. powdered stevia extract ✱
1/2 tsp. maple flavoring
1 tsp. vanilla extract
1 1/2 cups raw sesame seeds
1/3 cup w.w. flour
1/4 tsp. salt

Preheat oven to 375°. Oil a large baking pan (about 9 x 13-inch) or small cookie sheet with sides.

In a small bowl, blend the oil into the nut butter. If the nut butter is very thick use the larger amount of oil. If it is thin use the lesser amount. Mix in the apple butter, maple syrup, stevia extract, maple flavoring, and vanilla.

Place the sesame seeds in a large mixing bowl. Stir in the nut butter mixture. Add the flour and salt. Mix well.

Press the mixture evenly and firmly into the bottom of the dish or cookie sheet to about 1/4 inch thick. **Bake 15-18 minutes**.

Cool completely before cutting.

GRANOLA ENERGY BARS

2 tsp. powdered stevia leaf

2 cups granola (use your favorite-if it has chopped nuts and dried fruit all the better)

1/3 cup tahini, cashew, or almond butter

2 tbls. oil

1/3 cup apple butter

1 tbls. liquid Fruitsource or honey

1/3 tsp. stevia extract

1 tsp. vanilla

Preheat oven to 375°. Oil a 5 x 9-inch baking dish.

Mix the powdered stevia leaf into the granola in a large mixing bowl.

In a small bowl mix the nut butter and the oil together. Add the apple butter, Fruitsource (or honey), stevia extract, and vanilla. Gently stir this mixture into the granola.

Press the batter firmly and evenly into the baking dish. **Bake 18-20 minutes**. Cool completely before cutting.

OPTION: Add 1 heaping tablespoon protein powder to batter.

TROPICAL FRUIT BARS

CRUST

1/2 cup raw cashews (finely ground)
1/2 cup w.w. flour or barley flour
pinch of salt
1/4 tsp. powdered stevia extract ✳
3 tbls. oil

Preheat oven to 350°. Oil an 8-inch or 5 x 9-inch pan.

Grind the cashews in a blender. Mix the cashews, flour, salt, and stevia together in a bowl. Stir the oil in with a fork until it is evenly distributed. Press mixture firmly into the pan. **Bake for 12-15 minutes**. Cool.

MIDDLE LAYER

4 large dates (chopped)
1/4 cup water

Chop the dates and simmer in the water until a creamy paste (5-10 minutes). Add a little more water if too thick. Spread the date paste in a thin layer over the cooled crust.

FILLING

1 can crushed pineapple (8 ounces)
1 ripe banana (medium-sized)
1 tsp. vanilla extract
1/2 tsp. powdered stevia extract ✳
1/4 cup flour
1/2 cup unsweetened coconut

Reduce oven temperature to 325°.

In a blender cream the pineapple (with juice), banana, vanilla, and stevia together. Pour into a mixing bowl. Gently stir in the flour and coconut. Pour filling evenly over crust. **Bake 45-50 minutes** until knife inserted near edge comes out clean. Cool completely before cutting.

PEANUT BUTTER BARS

These are sure to please

1/2 cup peanut butter
1/3 cup oil
1/4 cup apple butter
2 tbls. date sugar
1/2 tsp. powdered stevia extract ✱
1 tsp. vanilla
1 ounce soft tofu OR 1 egg

1 cup w.w. pastry flour
1/2 cup rolled oats (quick cooking o.k.)
1/2 tsp. baking soda
1/4 tsp. salt

Preheat oven to 350°. Oil a 11 x 7-inch baking pan or similar size.

Mix the peanut butter and oil together in a bowl. If your peanut butter is already runny reduce oil added and increase peanut butter some. Mix in the apple butter, date sugar, stevia, vanilla, and tofu (or egg). Tofu may be blended first in a blender or creamed directly into the batter until smooth.

Stir in the flour, oats, baking soda, and salt. Press the batter into the bottom of the pan. **Bake 25 minutes.**

(over)

FROSTING

1/2 cup carob powder
3/4 cup milk
1/3 tsp. powdered stevia ✱
1/3 cup peanut butter
1 tsp. vanilla

Mix the carob, milk, and stevia together in a sauce pan. Heat on a low boil for about 7 minutes. Remove from heat and mix in peanut butter.

Remove bars from oven. Frost immediately. Cool before cutting.

NOTE: May use half carob and half cocoa (or 1 square of Baker's chocolate - melted) plus 2 tbls. honey.

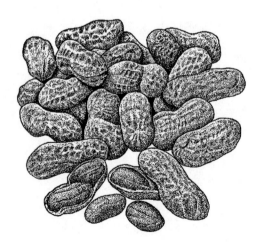

PUDDINGS
AND
PIES

CAROB PUDDING

Rich and silky smooth

1/2 cup carob syrup
12 ounces silken or soft tofu
1 tbls. oil
1/3 tsp. powdered stevia extract ✳
1 large banana
1/2 tsp. vanilla
pinch of salt

To make carob syrup place 1/2 cup carob powder and 1/2 cup water in a small heavy-bottomed pan. Cook at a low boil for 6-8 minutes, stirring constantly until thick and smooth. If too thick add a little more water.

Place all the ingredients in a blender and blend until creamy. Spoon in dessert dishes and chill in the refrigerator about 1 hour.

Serves: 4

CREAMY BAKED RICE PUDDING

Great to make on a cold day

1 tsp. butter or margarine
1/2 *cup short-grained brown rice (uncooked)*
3 cups milk
1/2 tsp. powdered stevia extract ✱
1/2 tsp. stevia concentrate ✪
1 tbls. lemon juice
finely grated rind of 1 lemon
1/4 cup raisins (optional)
1/2 tsp. cinnamon

Preheat to 300°. Butter a medium-sized casserole dish with the butter or margarine.

Place the uncooked rice in the casserole dish with half of the milk. Cover dish and place in oven.

After about 1 hour stir in the rest of the milk, the stevia extracts, lemon juice, rind, cinnamon, and raisins (if desired).

About every hour take casserole out of the oven and stir. **Bake about 3 1/2 to 4 hours** total until thick but creamy.

CHOCOLATE PUDDING

A smooth and sumptuous chocolate treat

1 1/2 squares Baker's chocolate
3 cups milk
2-3 tbls. corn starch
2-3 tbls. flour
3 tbls. honey or maple syrup
3/4 tsp. powdered stevia extract ✱
1 tbls. vanilla extract
pinch of salt

NOTE: If using the pudding as a pie filling use the larger amounts of corn starch and flour so it will set better.

Melt chocolate squares on low heat in a heavy-bottomed pan or double boiler. Stir in the honey (or maple syrup) and the stevia. Mix 2 cups of the milk into the chocolate. Add a pinch of salt. Heat the mixture to below the boiling point.

While heating the milk, dissolve the corn starch and flour in the remaining cup of milk. Smooth out any lumps. Gradually add the starches to the hot milk.

Cook on medium-low about 5 minutes until thick, stirring gently. Continue cooking on low 3-5 minutes longer. Remove from heat and stir in the vanilla.

If making a pie, cool pudding first then pour into a pre-baked 9-inch pie shell.

SWEET POTATO PIE

A basic recipe – may be made with sweet potatoes, squash, yams, or pumpkin

SINGLE 9-INCH CRUST

1/4 tsp. salt
1 cup w.w. pastry flour + 2 tbls. soy flour
4 tbls. soft soy or canola margarine
3 tbls. cold water

Preheat oven to 425°. Mix salt into flour. Cut margarine into flour with a pastry blender or fork until well distributed (like a coarse meal). Sprinkle the water in gradually while mixing the flour.

Form into a ball and roll out between two pieces of wax paper. Remove top sheet of paper and flip over into a pie pan. Remove other paper. Trim and flute edges. Prick crust with a fork.

Prebake crust for 10-12 minutes. Drop oven temperature to 350°.

FILLING

2 eggs (separated)
2 cups cooked and mashed sweet potato (packed)
1 cup milk
2 tbls. apple butter
1 1/2 tsp. stevia concentrate ✪
1 tsp. cinnamon
3/4 tsp. ginger
1/4 tsp. nutmeg
1/4 tsp. salt

Separate eggs. Set whites aside. Blend the yolks and all the rest of the ingredients together in a blender. Pour into a mixing bowl.

Beat egg whites until stiff. Fold the whites gently into the filling. Place batter in cooked pie shell. **Bake for 45 minutes** or until a knife inserted at the edge of the pie comes out clean.

PEAR CUSTARD PIE

CRUST

Preheat oven to 400°. Prepare a 9-inch single pie crust (see page 67 or use your own recipe). Prick crust with a fork a number of times and **bake at 400° for 10 minutes**. Remove from oven and reduce temperature to 350°.

FILLING

2 1/2 to 3 cups sliced pear (fresh or canned)
1 1/4 cups low-fat cottage cheese
1/3 cup milk
1 large egg
1 tsp. vanilla extract
1/2 tsp. powdered stevia extract ✱
2 tbls. flour
pinch of salt

Lay the pear slices in the pie shell. Blend the rest of ingredients together in a blender until smooth. Pour blender mix over pears. **Bake for 40 minutes**. Remove from oven.

TOPPING

1/2 cup w.w. flour
1 tsp. cinnamon
1 tbls. butter
3/4 tsp. stevia concentrate

Place flour in a small bowl. Stir in the cinnamon. Mix in the butter then the stevia concentrate until well distributed. Sprinkle evenly over top of the pie. Return to oven and **bake 15-20 minutes** longer.

Chill before serving.

BLUEBERRY PIE

Prepare a double crust (double the recipe on page 67 or use your own recipe. Top crust may be whole or latticed.

> *4 cups of blueberries*
> *4 tbls. quick tapioca*
> *2-3 tbls. date sugar or granular Fruitsource*
> *3/4 tsp. powdered stevia extract* ✻
> *1 tbls. lemon juice*
> *1 tbls. butter*

Preheat oven to 450°.

In a bowl mix the berries with the rest of the ingredients except the butter. Let the berry mixture set for 15 minutes.

If using frozen berries take them out to thaw before making the crust. They just have to be thawed enough so they're not clumped together.

Place berries in unbaked pie shell. Dot top with pieces of butter. Roll out the top crust. Cut for a latticed top or use whole with vents. Flute edge.

Bake at 450° for 10 minutes.
Reduce heat to 350° and **bake for 45 to 1 hour** until golden brown.

APPLE CRISP

FILLING

7-8 cups chopped apples (peeling optional)
3 tbls. lemon juice
1 tsp. vanilla
1 to 1 1/2 tsp. powdered stevia leaf 🍂
2 tbls. flour
3 tbls. peanut butter
1 tsp. cinnamon
1/4 tsp. salt
2/3 cups fruit juice

TOPPING

1 cup rolled oats
2/3 cups nuts and seeds (chopped)
1/4 tsp. powdered stevia extract ✳
3/4 tsp. stevia concentrate ✪
2 tbls. oil

Preheat oven to 350°. Butter a large baking dish (9 x 13-inch).

Place the chopped apples in a large mixing bowl. Stir in the lemon juice. Mix the vanilla, stevia leaf, flour, peanut butter, cinnamon, and salt into the apples.

Pour the fruit juice into the bottom of the dish. Spoon in the apple mixture.

Mix the oats, chopped nuts and seeds, stevia extract, and stevia concentrate together in a bowl. Sprinkle and stir in the oil. Spread the topping over the apples so it is evenly distributed.

Bake 50 minutes to 1 hour. If the topping gets done before the apples, cover pan with foil the last 15 minutes of baking.

GELATIN DESSERTS

APPLE MOUSSE

2 cups unsweetened apple juice (filtered)
2 tbls. agar-agar OR 1 pkg. gelatin
1/4 tsp. powdered stevia extract ✳
1 tsp. vanilla extract
1-2 tbls. cashew butter or tahini

Combine the juice and agar-agar in a small pan. Bring to a boil and reduce to a simmer. Simmer 4-5 minutes until agar is dissolved. Remove from the heat and stir in the stevia extract and vanilla.

Pour into a shallow dish and chill several hours until set.

Remove from refrigerator. Break up agar with a spatula and place in a blender. Puree on low speed until creamy. Blend in the cashew butter or tahini. Spoon into custard cups and serve immediately.

Serves: 4

NOTE: If using gelatin, sprinkle gelatin over 1/2 cup cold juice. Soften about 5 minutes. Simmer on low until gelatin is dissolved. Mix in the stevia. Pour rest of juice in a dish. Mix in dissolved gelatin. Refrigerate until set. Remove from refrigerator. Break up and place in blender. Blend with nut butter until smooth. Return to refrigerator until set.

FRUIT JUICE GELATIN

4 cups unsweetened fruit juice (filtered)
4 tbls. agar-agar OR 2 pkgs. gelatin
1/2 tsp. powdered stevia extract ✱
1 cup fruit (optional)

Suggested juices: apple or white grape juice blend with raspberry or strawberry, peach or pear blends.

Place juice in a sauce pan with the agar. Bring the juice to a boil and then reduce to a simmer. Simmer 4-5 minutes until agar is dissolved. Mix in the stevia.

Place fresh, frozen, or canned (drained) fruit into the bottom of a dish or mold. May use bananas, berries, pears, or peaches. Pour juice mixture over fruit. Refrigerate until set.

VARIATION: Break up the gel and place in a blender. Blend with one to two cups of whipped cream or soft tofu until creamy. Serve immediately.

NOTE: If using gelatin sprinkle gelatin over 1 cup cold juice. Soften about 5 minutes. Simmer over low until dissolved. Mix in the stevia. In a bowl place the rest of the juice. Mix in the dissolved gelatin. Refrigerate until the consistency of egg whites. Remove from refrigerator and add fruit if desired or blend in whipped cream then add fruit. Return to refrigerator until set.

CRANBERRY GELATIN SALAD

12 ounces frozen unsweetened cran-apple juice
concentrate (thawed)
2 1/2 cups water
1/2 cup grapes (halved)
3/4 cup red apple (chopped, not peeled)
1/2 cup chopped cranberries
1/4 cup chopped walnuts (optional)
2 pkgs. gelatin OR 4 tbls. agar-agar
1 tbls. lemon juice
3/4 tsp. powdered stevia extract ✳

Chop grapes and apples. Sprinkle with lemon juice and set aside. Chop cranberries (may use a blender). Mix some of the stevia into the cranberries. Set aside. Chop the nuts.

Place 1/2 cup of juice concentrate and 1/2 cup of water in a pan. Sprinkle the gelatin on top. Soften the gelatin about 5 minutes. Simmer on low until gelatin is dissolved. Mix in rest of stevia.

In a bowl mix together the rest of the juice and water. Add the dissolved gelatin. Place bowl in refrigerator until partly set (the consistency of egg whites).

When gelatin is partly set, mix in the fruit and nuts. Spoon into individual serving bowls or into a single mold and return to the refrigerator to re-set.

Serves: 8-10

NOTE: If using agar-agar, heat all of the juice and water in a pan. Add agar and bring to a boil. Reduce heat and simmer for about 5 minutes until agar is completely dissolved. Stir in the stevia. Place the fruit and nuts in a dish and pour the juice mixture over it. Chill in the refrigerator several hours.

SPARKLING GELATIN

12 ounces unsweetened apple-raspberry juice
concentrate (thawed)
1/2 cup water
2 pkgs. gelatin
1/2 tsp. powdered stevia extract ✳
2 cups carbonated water
2 cups raspberries

Place 1/2 cup juice concentrate and 1/2 cup water in a small pan. Sprinkle gelatin over surface. Let stand 5 minutes then cook over low until gelatin is dissolved. Mix in the stevia.

In a bowl add the rest of the concentrate, carbonated water, and the dissolved gelatin. Refrigerate until partly set (the consistency of egg whites). Stir in the berries. Pour into a mold or individual serving bowls. Return to refrigerator until firmly set.

Serves: 8

NOTE: Agar-agar doesn't set when using carbonated water.

TOPPINGS
AND
SAUCES

APPLESAUCE

METHOD I

6 cups chopped apples (peeled and cored)
3 cups water
1 1/2 tsp. cinnamon
3/4 tsp. powdered stevia extract ✳
1/2 tsp. stevia concentrate (optional) ✪

Blend apples and water together in a blender-2 cups of apples to 1 cup of water at a time. Pour into a sauce pan and cook over medium-low heat. Add the cinnamon and stevia. Cook until heated through and until sauce is of desired thickness.

Yield: About 1 quart

METHOD II

8-10 cups chopped apples
1 1/2 tsp. cinnamon
3/4 tsp. powdered stevia extract ✳
1/2 tsp. stevia concentrate (optional) ✪

Don't peel or core the apples but cut out bad spots. Cover apples with water in a large pot. Boil down the apples about 45 minutes to an hour. Stir occasionally and add more water if necessary. Cook until apples are completely softened.

Remove from the heat and push the apples through a sieve or strainer. Keep pressing until only the peels and cores are left. Return to pan and stir in the cinnamon and stevia.

If canning follow standard procedures. Sterilize the jars and lids. Return sauce to a boil. Pour sauce into jars and cover.

Yield: About 1 quart

APPLE BUTTER

1 quart of unsweetened applesauce
apple juice
cinnamon to taste (about 1 1/2 tsp.)
powdered stevia extract to taste (about 1/2 tsp.) ✳
1/2 tsp. stevia concentrate (optional) ✪

Pour applesauce in a heavy-bottomed pan. If using homemade sauce, the sauce made by method II on page 77 works best.

Boil the sauce on low for several hours stirring occasionally. Periodically adding some apple juice or cider will make the apple butter creamier and richer but will take longer to thicken.

Add cinnamon and stevia to taste. Cook until sauce is reduced in half or more until desired thickness is reached.

NOTE: If your sauce is already sweetened with stevia, you will probably not need to add all of the 1/2 tsp. called for.

PLUM SAUCE

2 cups chopped plums (pitted)
water to cover
1/4 tsp. powdered stevia extract ✳

Chop plums and remove pits. Place in sauce pan and cover with water. Cook about one hour until soft.

NOTE: Some plums are hard and will take longer to cook than soft ones. Both hard and soft plums work well making a wonderfully rich red sauce.

Once completely softened, remove from the heat and strain through a sieve or strainer. Return to the pan. Add the stevia and cook sauce until desired thickness.

For pouring over pancakes, etc. use a thinner sauce.

For spreading the sauce on toast or in crepes make a thicker sauce

APRICOT SAUCE

1 cup dried apricots
unsweetened apple juice to cover plus 1 cup
1 tsp. stevia concentrate ✪ OR
1/2 tsp. powdered stevia extract ✳
1 tbls. arrowroot powder
pinch of salt

Simmer apricots in juice until very tender about 45 minutes. Periodically add more juice as necessary to keep apricots covered.

Place cooked apricots in a blender with the cup of apple juice, stevia concentrate, arrowroot, and salt. Process until smooth. Add a little extra juice if apricots are still too thick to blend. Return to pan and cook over low several minutes until thickened. Serve warm or cold.

CHOCOLATE SAUCE

6 level tbls. cocoa
1 tsp. powdered stevia extract ✱
1 cup milk
4 tbls. honey
1 tsp. vanilla extract
1 tbls. butter

In a small pan, stir the stevia into the cocoa. Cream in about half of the milk. Bring to a light boil. Add the honey. Gradually stir in the rest of the milk while mixture is boiling. Boil 2-3 minutes. Remove from heat. Beat in the vanilla and butter.

Serve warm or cold over ice cream.

Yield: about 1 cup

APPLE FILLING

3 cups chopped apples (peeled & cored)
water to cover
1 cup apple juice
2 tbls. lemon juice
1 1/2 tbls. cornstarch OR 2 tbls. arrowroot or kudzu
1/3 tsp. powdered stevia extract ✸
12 tsp. cinnamon
14 tsp. nutmeg

Place 1 cup of the apples in a medium-sized sauce pan. Cover with water and begin cooking the apples.

While apples are cooking place other 2 cups of apples in a blender with the rest of the ingredients.

When the water is nearly gone in pan add the blender mix. Bring to a boil then cook on low 20-30 minutes stirring occasionally until mixture is thick and apple pieces are tender.

The sauce gets much thicker upon cooling. Excellent for crepes, pancakes, and turnovers.

VARIATION: Also works great with pears.

BERRY PANCAKE SYRUP

1 cup fresh or frozen berries
1/2 cup unsweetened apple juice or apple blend
1/2 tsp. powdered stevia extract ✱
1 tbls. quick tapioca

Blend all the ingredients together in a blender. Pour into a sauce pan. Cook just until a full boil is reached, then remove from the heat.

Tapioca thickens as it cools. Serve warm.

JAM

1 1/2 quarts fresh berries
1 cup unsweetened fruit juice concentrate
Pomona's Universal Pectin*
3/4 tsp. powdered stevia extract ✶

Follow directions provided in package of Pomona's Universal Pectin. Pomona's pectin can be used with sugar, honey, fruit juice, artificial sweetener, or stevia.

• Wash, rinse, and sterilize jars.
• Clean berries, remove hulls, and mash. One and one half quarts of fresh berries will be 3 cups mashed. Place in a sauce pan.
• Add 4 tsp. calcium water to berries and stir well.
• In another small sauce pan bring the juice concentrate to a boil. Place in a blender. Add 2 tsp. of pectin powder and blend 1-2 minutes until powder is dissolved.
• Bring fruit to a boil. Add the dissolved pectin. Stir vigorously 1 minute. Stir in the stevia extract. Bring back to a boil and remove from heat.
• Fill jars to 1/2-inch from the top. Screw on 2-piece lids. Boil 5 minutes. Remove from water and let jars cool. Lids should pop to be sealed.

*To purchase Pomona's
see page 103.

Pomona's Jam Hotline:
(413)772-6816

FROZEN DESSERTS

❖ MAKING FROZEN DESSERTS ❖

ELECTRIC AUTOMATIC: There are several brands of wonderful electric ice cream machines on the market today that don't require salt or ice. I bought a Cuisinart brand that works extremely well. The container is kept in the freezer overnight. The walls contain a substance that freezes. Simply plug in the machine and pour in the blended ingredients (only chill the ingredients first if they were cooked on the stove). The ice cream is ready in about 30 minutes. TIP: After the ice cream is ready, remove the paddle, pack the ice cream down in the container, wrap a towel around it and place it in the refrigerator for about 30 minutes to 1 1/2 hours to harden before serving. This will insure the best consistency. However, if you leave it too long the ice cream will get too hard and dry. Pack the left over in a covered container. Thaw about 15 minutes before serving again.

ELECTRIC CHURNED: This machine requires alternating the outer container with layers of crushed ice and rock salt. Chill the mixture before pouring into the freezer can. When done harden the ice cream for better texture by re-packing the container with ice and salt, remove paddle, pack down the ice cream and wrap up the machine. Keep covered about 2-3 hours for best texture.

HAND CHURNED: Follow directions for electric churned that is packed in rock salt and ice. You do the work.

REFRIGERATOR METHOD: Prepare the mixture like above. Pour into a freezer tray or any flat pan. Freeze until mushy but not solid (about 1-2 hrs.). Place in a chilled bowl and beat with chilled beaters until smooth. Work quickly. Return mixture to tray and freeze hard. Remove from freezer. Soften about 10 to 15 minutes then beat in a blender or food processor until a smooth texture is achieved. Pack into covered containers and re-freeze. Before serving, soften for about 15 minutes if necessary.

FROZEN FRUIT YOGURT

2 cups plain yogurt
1 cup fresh fruit or frozen (thawed)
1/2 cup frozen unsweetened apple juice
concentrate (thawed)
2 tbls. frozen orange juice concentrate (thawed)
3/4 tsp. powdered stevia extract ✱
1 tsp. vanilla

Blend all ingredients together in a blender. If using raspberries or blackberries, press the blended ingredients through a strainer to remove seeds.

Pour contents into the container of the ice cream machine. Process according to directions.

CHOCOLATE ICE CREAM

1 1/2 squares Baker's chocolate
3 tbls. honey
3/4 tsp. powdered stevia extract ✱
1 tsp. vanilla
1 1/2 cups milk
1-12 ounce pkg. silken tofu

Melt the chocolate over low heat in a heavy-bottomed pan. Stir in the honey, and several ounces of the milk. Boil on low for 2-3 minutes. Add the rest of the milk and the vanilla.

Blend the chocolate mixture, tofu, and stevia together in a blender until smooth. If still warm, chill the mixture in the refrigerator before pouring it in the ice cream maker.

Process according to the directions of your ice cream machine.

NOTE: May replace the tofu and milk with 2 cups half and half and 1 cup whole milk.

MAPLE NUT ICE CREAM

2 cups half & half
1 cup milk
2 tbls. maple syrup
1/2 tsp. maple flavoring
3/4 tsp. powdered stevia extract ✳
1/2 cup chopped walnuts

Blend all the ingredients together except the nuts. Pour into an ice cream machine and process. Add the chopped walnuts about half way into the freezing process. Nuts should be no bigger in size than a chocolate chip.

VARIATION: For **Vanilla Ice Cream** use

2 cups half & half
1 cup milk
1–2 tbls. honey
3/4-1 tsp. powdered stevia extract✳
1 tbls. vanilla extract

Blend all the ingredients together in a blender. Pour into the container of an ice cream machine and process according to directions. If using less honey use the larger amount of stevia. The texture is better with the larger amount of honey.

NOTE: The two recipes above do not work well when using yogurt or tofu– the flavor is poor.

89

RASPBERRY SHERBET

This is absolutely delicious!

2 cups plain yogurt
1/4 cup milk
1/2 cup unsweetened raspberry juice blend concentrate (thawed)
1 tbls. orange juice concentrate or blend (thawed)
1 tsp. vanilla extract
3/4 tsp. powdered stevia extract *
1 banana (optional)

Blend all the ingredients together in a blender until smooth.

Pour into the container of the ice cream machine and process according to directions.

NOTE: It works very well to substitute the yogurt for a 12-ounce package of silken tofu. Add a total of 1 cup of milk.

May use any fruit juice blend concentrate of your choice.

QUICK BERRY ICE CREAM

6 frozen bananas
2 cups frozen berries
1 cup plain yogurt
1/2 tsp. powdered stevia extract ✳

Slice frozen bananas into blender or food processor. (To freeze bananas peel first and place in an airtight bag in the freezer.) Place the rest of ingredients into the blender or food processor. If using a blender, use the pulse button. Between pulses stir the mixture. Process until smooth. Serve immediately.

Serves: 8

❖ INGREDIENTS GLOSSARY ❖

AGAR-AGAR   Flakes or bars derived from sea algae. Used as a gelling agent in place of animal gelatin. It supplies bulk and lubrication in the intestinal tract and increases peristaltic action, thus relieving constipation.

ALMONDS   The fruit of a small tree related to the peach. High in protein, B vitamins, and the minerals: calcium, phosphorus, and iron. This healthful nut can be made into almond butter, almond milk, or ground into a meal.

APPLE BUTTER   The pulp of apples, cooked, strained, and cooked further until thick and creamy. Several unsweetened brands are available.

ARROWROOT POWDER   A starch from the tuberous roots of a tropical American plant used as a thickening agent in sauces and puddings. It is high in minerals and easily digested. Can be substituted for corn starch. Basic proportions are 1 tbls. of arrowroot to 1 cup of liquid.

BRAN   The outer layers of grain. It absorbs moisture, providing bulk in the intestinal tract. Oat and wheat bran are most often used. Absorbs liquid in baked goods, as well, which may lead to a dry or crumbly product if too much is added.

BROWN RICE   Whole, unpolished rice. Not separated from its bran and germ as white rice is.

BUTTERMILK   Originally this was the residue from the butter churn. Today it is generally made from pasteurized skim milk with a culture added to produce a heavier consistency and to develop the flavor.

CAROB POWDER Finely ground pod of the tamarind, also called St. John's Bread. An excellent bowel conditioner, it is also high in minerals, very alkaline and rich in natural sugars. Used as an alternative to chocolate.

CASHEW The cashew nut is the seed of the cashew apple, which grows on the outside of the fruit. A tropical American tree of the Sumac Family, cashews are a good source of vitamin D and B1 (thiamine), iron, protein, and unsaturated fats. This soft, versatile nut can be blended to a smooth white liquid that replaces dairy products as milk, cream, and whipped cream. It also can be processed into an excellent nut butter.

CORN STARCH A fine powder derived from the endosperm of the corn kernel. Used for thickening sauces and puddings. Causes digestive problems and allergic reactions in some.

CRANBERRIES The tart berries of a shrub related to blueberries (*Vaccinium*), native to the bog habitat of eastern North America but now grown commercially in ponds.

DATE SUGAR Dehydrated and pulverized dates.

EGGS Use eggs from free-running or cage-free chickens if possible. Chickens suffer tremendously on large commercial farms.

EGG REPLACER A powdered product is available consisting of potato starch, tapioca flour, leavening, and vegetable gums. Also, tofu, nut butters, apple butter, and banana act as binders in a recipe.

FLOUR Wheat flour's superb rising ability is due to its high gluten content. This quality has made wheat flour the norm for bakers. A number of other flours are available that may be used, in whole or in part, to add flavor and variety to baked goods. Some flours may produce a heavier dough and more leavening may be required. I recommend using whole grain flours as much as possible. Enriched white flours only replace several of the 20 or more nutrients removed with the germ in refining flour. Whole grain flours should be refrigerated to maintain freshness. *(continued on next page)*

•**Amaranth** – The seed of an ancient plant used by the Aztecs. A nutritionally superior food that can be ground into a flour.

•**Barley** - Smooth, mild-flavored and a very good substitute for wheat flour. Contains a small amount of gluten.

•**Corn** - Ground whole kernel corn, finer than corn meal.

•**Oat** - May buy oat flour or grind from toasted flakes (see page 12). Use in small amounts as a dry product may result.

•**Quinoa** – The seed of an ancient Andean plant related to spinach. A nutritional superfood, delicately flavored, that may be used whole like millet or ground into a flour.

•**Rice** - Finely ground rice. Has a gritty quality. See page 14.

•**Soy** - High in protein, it boosts the protein complement in food. Never eat uncooked because it contains an enzyme that blocks digestion. Toasted soy flour can be purchased. Soy flour is also 20% fat. It's strong flavor restricts use to no more than 25% of the total flour in a recipe. Soy flour provides a tender, moist, and nicely browned product.

•**Spelt** - A variety of hard wheat tolerated by those allergic to regular wheat flours.

•**Wheat** - Available in hard and soft varieties and further classified as spring or winter wheat, referring to the season in which they are planted. Hard wheats have a high gluten content that are best for baking bread. These are called *whole wheat*, with stone-ground whole wheat being the coarsest but retaining the most nutrients. Soft wheats are ground into *pastry flour*. They are low in gluten and do not rise as well. However, they are finer and more suitable for baking. Whole wheat pastry flour is recommended. *Unbleached white flour* is refined and enriched but has not been put through a bleaching process. It can be used when a lighter, finer texture is desired.

FRUITSOURCE   A brand-name granular or liquid sweetener derived from grapes and rice.

GELATIN   An animal by-product used for gelling liquids.

HONEY   Produced by bees from the nectar of flowers. Nearly twice as sweet as sugar. Use moderately.

LEAVENINGS   Quick rising can be accomplished by using baking soda or baking powder. Baking soda (sodium bicarbonate) interacts with acidic ingredients like buttermilk, yogurt, fruit juices, vinegar, molasses and honey. Carbon dioxide bubbles are released that are locked into place by heat.

Baking powders contain both the alkaline and the acidic components; usually sodium bicarbonate with either tartaric acid, calcium acid phosphate, or sodium aluminum sulfate. These compounds interact to form carbon dioxide. Tartaric acid powders are single acting with the action taking place in the cold batter. See page 12 for making your own baking powder.

Double-acting baking powders start work in the cold dough and have additional rising action in the heat of the oven. Phosphate powders are double acting, but most of their action takes place in the cold batter. Most of the action of aluminum powders takes place in a hot oven. They are more effective, but for health reasons, aluminum-free baking powders are recommended.

In recipes containing acid ingredients, both baking powder and baking soda are often used. A small amount of soda is needed to neutralize the acid and less baking powder is required.

Keep leavenings to a minimum; generally no more than 1 tsp. per cup of flour.

LECITHIN   Phosphatides extracted primarily from soybeans. Emulsifies cholesterol in the blood, breaks up fats into small particles, and regulates the deposit of fat in the liver. May be added to baked goods and other foods.

MAPLE SYRUP   The boiled down, concentrated sap of the maple tree. Use genuine maple syrup.

MAPLE FLAVORING   A concentrated natural flavoring in a glycerin base. Imitation flavoring not recommended.

MEAL   Coarsely ground grains, nuts, and seeds. Easier to digest than whole nuts.

MARGARINE Some of the recipes call for butter or margarine. Most margarines are considered harmful to the health due to the presence of trans-fatty acids. A new margarine is now available called Earth Balance that is hardened by the addition of some palm oil. The naturally hard oils (palm, coconut) are no longer considered unhealthy. If you prefer margarine to butter this may be a good choice. Another brand, Caneleo, has 16% trans-fatty acids. I can tolerate this margarine over others of its type.

MOLASSES *Blackstrap* molasses is a by-product of the early stages of white sugar refinement, rich in minerals especially iron and calcium. Blackstrap molasses is more a flavoring agent than a sweetener. *Barbados* molasses is also made from sugar cane but it is not a by-product. The juice of the sugar cane is extracted, filtered, and boiled down to a syrup. The mineral content is low compared to blackstrap. It is the starting substance for making rum. *Sorghum* molasses is made in a similar way to Barbados molasses but is made from another grass species, sorghum, instead of sugar cane.

OIL Cold-pressed oils retain their nutrients. Safflower and canola oil are mild-flavored, all-purpose oils containing over 90% polyunsaturated fats. Corn oil is strong-flavored and heavy. Sunflower oil has a slightly sweet and buttery taste and contains about 60% polyunsaturated fats. Store oils (except olive oil) in the refrigerator to retain freshness.

PEANUT BUTTER the seeds of a legume that ripen in a pod underground. Use unhydrogenated natural peanut butter for baking.

POPPYSEEDS This seed comes from a different species than the opium poppy. Seeds may be roasted, steamed, or crushed to release more flavor.

RICE MILK A naturally sweet, pleasant-tasting, and low-fat extraction of brown rice. In my experience, rice milk will not thicken with corn starch or arrowroot powder.

SESAME TAHINI A butter made from ground white sesame seeds. It is 45% protein and 55% unsaturated oils. A nutritious and versatile substitute for a number of dairy products.

SUNFLOWER SEEDS A nutritious and economical substitute for nuts. Packed with magnesium, calcium, phosphorus, and unsaturated fats. Can be blended with nuts to make milk.

SOY MILK A beverage made from soybeans that can be substituted in equal parts for dairy milk. May be high in fat, so read the label. It works well in puddings. Can be purchased in convenient vacuum-packed carton with a long shelf-life.

TOFU A white curd made from soybeans and a coagulant in a process similar to cheese making. An inexpensive and versatile source of protein. It is measured by weight in the following recipes.

VANILLA An extract of the seed pod of a tropical American climbing orchid.

YOGURT Cow's milk cultured with bacteria that is beneficial to the intestinal tract. Also available from goat's milk and soy milk.

ZEST The colored, outer portion of oranges, tangerines, lemons and limes. Contain high concentrations of flavorful oils. Avoid grating the bitter white layer underneath.

SEA SALT Sea water which has been vacuum dried at low temperatures. Contains all the sea water minerals.

SESAME SEEDS The seed of an herb that grows in India. Very high in magnesium, calcium, lecithin, and amino acids. Yields a flavorful oil high in unsaturated fats. Makes a nutritious milk suitable for children.

❖ USEFUL EQUIPMENT ❖

Basting Brush   For applying butter and glazes to pie or bread crust.

Blender (Multi-speed) or Food Processor - Indispensable. I've had the same 10-speed Osterizer blender for nearly 20 years.

Hand Blender   The high-speed Braun is useful for blender drinks, sauces, and dressings. Convenient and less clean-up time.

Cheese Cloth For separating liquid from pulp.

Colander For washing and draining fruits and vegetables.

Cookie Cutters

Cooling Racks   To cool baked goods whether in the pan or out. Circulates air for faster cooling.

Cutting Boards   Have a separate board for cutting fruit and working with bread or cookie batter. This will keep them from absorbing onion and garlic odors. If made from wood, the boards must be scoured periodically with lemon, baking soda, or bleach.

Graters 4-sided grater, wooden ginger grater.

Grater Brush A small wire brush. Makes a frustrating job easy.

Grinders   Nut grinder, nutmeg grinder if you like to use fresh whole nutmeg.

Juicer Squeeze citrus by using a hand juicer or an electric one.

Measuring Cups and Spoons Graduated glass cups in 1 and 2 cup sizes, and larger if desired. Stainless steel or plastic nesting cup set. Two metal or plastic nesting measuring spoon sets.

Mixing Bowls   Several large, medium, and small, but deep, bowls. Either glass, ceramic, or stainless steel. Lighter weight bowls are more practical.

Mixer   Small electric hand mixers are helpful in making cakes, whipping eggs, and making frosting.

Oven Thermometer   Oven temperatures may differ from the gauge. Some thermometers also are not accurate, but I prefer to use one.

Pastry Blender   For cutting fat into flour.

Pastry Cloth and Cover for Rolling Pin   Helpful in reducing the introduction of too much flour when rolling out refrigerator cookies and pie crusts.

Pot Holders   Gloves or pads-nice thick ones.

Rolling Pin   For rolling out pie crusts and cookie dough.

Sifter   For thoroughly combining dry ingredients. Use a triple sifter. Never wash a sifter.

Spatulas   Rubber spatulas for cleaning out the blender and the bowl.   A straight-edge wooden spatula works well for stirring puddings.

Strainers   A fine-mesh tea strainer for straining the pulp and seeds from citrus fruit. A hand-held 5-inch fine-mesh strainer.

Timer   Never forget again!

Whisks   For whipping eggs and combining liquid ingredients.

Wooden Spoons   Solid and slotted.

BAKEWARE

The choice of baking pans makes a difference in the baking temperature, baking times, and the quality of the finished product.

Dark bakeware and glass absorb and hold heat. Therefore, food cooked in such pans need to bake at a 10° to 25° lower temperature than food cooked in shiny metal pans which deflect heat. If the food is cooking too fast, it will brown quickly on the outside but not get done on the inside. When using dark bakeware, watch the item closely near the end of its baking time. Cover with foil if surface is getting too brown.

Heavier bakeware is better because it absorbs, retains, and distributes heat evenly. Light-weight cake pans and cookie sheets have dead or hot spots. You may double-pan a thin cake pan.

There is evidence that aluminum from non-anodized aluminum cookware dissolves into food and causes a whole range of health problems. Non-anodized aluminum cookware is banned in some countries. But in the U.S., it is widely used in homes, restaurants, and in the processed food industry. Choose an alternate material when possible. Below is a list of recommended bakeware.

2 round 8-inch cake pans
1 9-inch Tube or Bundt pan (8 or 10 inch o.k.)
1 8-inch Spring-form pan
1 9-inch Spring-form pan
1 8-inch square baking pan
1 5x9-inch baking pan
1 11x7-inch baking pan
1 9x13-inch glass baking pan
2 loaf pans
2 muffin pans
2 cookie sheets
2 9-inch pie pans
1 9-inch glass deep dish pie pan

❖ MEASURES ❖

1 tablespoon	=	3 teaspoons
2 tablespoons	=	1 ounce
4 tablespoons	=	1/4 cup or 2 ounces
5 1/3 tablespoons	=	1/3 cup or 2 2/3 ounces
8 tablespoons	=	1/2 cup or 4 ounces
16 tablespoons	=	1 cup or 8 ounces
1 pint	=	2 cups or 16 ounces
1 quart	=	2 pints or 32 ounces
1 gallon	=	4 quarts

❖ RESOURCES ❖

COOKBOOKS

Below is a list of cookbooks that gave me inspiration or were instructional. I thank all these bakers for their hard work and contribution to wholesome cooking.

Naturally Delicious Desserts and Snacks by Faye Martin, Rodale Press, Emmaus, PN, 1978.

The Book of Whole Meals by Annemarie Colbin, Ballantine Books, New York, 1979.

Sweet and Sugarfree by Karen E. Barkie, St. Martin's Press, New York, 1982.

Desserts to Lower Your Fat Thermostat by Barbara W. Higa, Vitality House International, Inc., Provo, Utah, l988.

Sweet & Natural Desserts a compilation from the Editors of East West Journal, l986.

The American Vegetarian Cookbook from the Fit for Life Kitchen by Marilyn Diamond.

The Ten Talents Cookbook by Frank and Rosalie Hurd, The College Press, Collegedale, TN, 1968.

The New Laurel's Kitchen by Laurel Robertson, Carol Flinders and Brian Ruppenthal, Ten Speed Press, Berkeley, CA, 1986.

The Joy of Cooking by Irma Rombauer and Marion Rombauer Becker, Penguin Putnam, Inc., New York, NY, 1997.

Great Cakes by Carole Walter.

Tofu Cookery by Louise Hagler, the Book Publishing Co., Summertown, TN, 1982.

BAKING EQUIPMENT SOURCES

Williams-Sonoma Company, San Francisco, CA
1-800-541-1262   Free catalog

Bridge Kitchenware, New York, NY
1-212-688-4220   Catalog $3

Sweet Celebrations, Minneapolis, MN
1-800-328-6722   Free catalog

BOOKS ABOUT STEVIA

The Stevia Story by Linda Bonvie, Bill Bonvie & Donna Gates
The history, politics and uses of stevia, with recipes.

Stevia: Nature's Sweet Secret by David Richard
Information and recipes.

PRODUCT DIRECTORY

Fruitsource: distributed by Advanced Ingredients, Inc., 1803 Mission St., Suite 404, Santa Cruz, CA 95060 (831)464-9891

Maple Flavoring: The Spicery Shoppe, Donners Grove, IL 60515 (630)932-8100

Agar-agar: Imported by Eden Foods, Inc., Clinton, MI 49236 (517)456-7424

Kosher gelatin: Emes Kosher Products, Lombard IL 60148

Pomona's Universal Pectin: P.O. Box 1083, Greenfield, MA 01302 (413)772-6816

Earth Balance Natural Margarine: GFA Brands, Inc., P.O. Box 397, Cresskill, NJ 07626-0397 (201) 568-9300

Canoleo 100% Canola Margarine: Distributed by Spring Tree Corp., Brattleboro, VT 05302 (802)254-8784

MAKING LIQUID
STEVIA EXTRACT

Bring 2 cups of purified water to a boil. Reduce
heat to medium and add 1/4 cup of crushed or
powdered dried stevia leaves. Cover and boil for 3
minutes. Remove pan from the heat, cover and steep
the herb until the liquid cools. Pour the liquid
extract off from the settled herbs in the bottom of
the pan, then strain through a cheesecloth. Keep in a
covered container in the refrigerator. **The extract
will be dark greenish black in color.**

$$5 \text{ drops} = 2 \text{ tbls. sugar}$$
$$20 \text{ drops} = 1/2 \text{ cup sugar}$$
$$3/4 \text{ tsp.} = 1 \text{ cup sugar}$$

For a **cold extraction** soak 1/4 cup of powdered
leaf in 2 cups of water for 8 to 12 hours on the
counter. Strain through a cheesecloth. Refrigerate.

To make a stronger concentrate (from either method
above), let the tea stand several minutes then pour
liquid extract off from the sediment in the bottom.
Simmer the liquid in an uncovered pan on the stove
until reduced by half. Refrigerate. Concentrate will
be twice as strong.

❖ ORDERING INFORMATION ❖

TO ORDER BOOKS CALL: 1-805-645-5309

OR WRITE TO: Sun Coast Enterprises
PO Box 262
Oak View, CA 93022

Baking with Stevia, Recipes for the Sweet Leaf
Baking with Stevia II, More Recipes for the Leaf

Single copy $12.95
Two copies.....................$10.00 each
One of Each Volume...........$10.00 each

Discount prices are available when purchasing quantities of books from Sun Coast Enterprises. For a price list and shipping rates call the number above.

Shipping & Handling

Inside USA.................$2 for one copy, $3 for two copies
California residents add 7.25% sales tax
Make checks payable to Sun Coast Enterprises

SOURCES OF STEVIA PRODUCTS

Wisdom of the Ancients: *South American herbs, stevia products*
1-800-899-9908   Free catalog

Sweetvia Brands: *Stevia extract, books*
1-888-8-STEVIA or www.sweetvia.com

Jean's Greens: *Herbs, herbal products and books*
1-888-845-8327   Free catalog

Herbal Advantage, Inc.: *Stevia products and other herbs*
1-800-753-9906   Free catalog

Carolee's Herb Farm, Hartford City, IN   1-765-348-3162

ABOUT THE AUTHOR

Rita DePuydt is a free-lance botanist, gardener and writer/ photographer, originally from Michigan, now living in California. She also has a background in Home-Economics and as a Medical Laboratory Technician.

Health and healing herbs have been an interest of hers for several decades. She was a leader in a nutrition education and activist group during her college years, was on the education committee of her local food coop for several years, and has taught whole food cooking classes.

Rita has been dealing with sugar addiction since a child. Following numerous ups and downs, she became interested in stevia as a way of reducing her consumption of sugars and is experimenting with the herb to discover if it helps balance her blood sugar levels and reduce her sugar cravings.

Rita is now learning that it's worthwhile to focus on what you want not on what you don't want – to align your thoughts and feelings with what you really want. She believes that total health and happiness is within reach if you keep the vision and focus on the positive aspects.